May Go... ...
bless every thing,
read, every
have and every prayer y...

In Christ

To Karen, Barret, Nick, Craig,
Sharon, Amy, Megan,
Claire, Lucy, Allie and Parker
Without whom this would not have been possible.

And to the good people of the following
United Methodist Churches:
Lakewood, Northlawn, Wagarville, Woodenshoe,
The Gathering, New Hope, Millville, Peace
and Quimby. For all I learned with you and all you
loved me through.

CONTENTS

INTRODUCTION:

John Wesley, the 18th century founder of the Methodist Movement, developed a list of Christian practices as a guide for effective, growing Christian life. Consisting of seven regular disciplines the list has become widely known as *Wesley's Means of Grace* although many in the list have long since ceased to be a regular practice for many Christians. The list includes: The public worship of God – The ministry of the Word, either read or expounded – The Lord's Supper – Family and private prayer – Searching the Scriptures – Fasting and abstinence – and Christian conferencing. While this book will not help perfect every discipline on Wesley's list, it is hoped that perhaps the reader will find encouragement for each of them. In this book you may open it daily and take a brief look at the Scripture followed by some, hopefully, thought provoking stories and finally end your time with a prayer. My prayer is: you will be encouraged to go deeper in every sense, deeper into the Scripture, deeper into the story that is your life, and deeper into prayer for yourself, your friends and certainly your family.

You will notice some days are short and sweet, others a bit more involved, use each day as you see fit. The first half of this volume was written during a sabbatical/renewal leave prior to which I received a diagnosis of prostate cancer. I took several weeks to re-center my heart on God's Spirit and the result is this work. The second half of this volume was written during my recovery from surgery. Praise God from whom all blessing flow for many things, not the least of which is our modern medical procedures as volumes 2-4 will be forth coming. Please enjoy your walks in the garden alongside the rivers of living water in Eden.

Day 1:

"I've told you these things to prepare you for rough times ahead..." Jn 16:1 (MSSG)

There is nothing God has not warned us of. We may live our lives in a state of self-absorbed abundance, and from time to time experience challenges, or even tragedy and think God never warned us but the reality is, the Bible speaks to us.

For example, the story of the Prodigal in Luke 15, the father in this story is no different from any father raising children. His children are growing and exploring life, even while still under his care. He makes certain commitments to leave all he acquires to his children, a commitment made before God. So, even though a cultural norm for the time, this father has the integrity to stand by his decision and effectively becomes a steward of the estate on behalf of his children. When the younger son comes to him and asks for his share the father does not hesitate, he gives him his share of the estate. What follows is a very difficult journey, a period of "rough times," just as we would expect.

Well, what about our lives, how many parents today have experienced a prodigal in the lives, how many parents today were the prodigals in their family? Jesus may have been speaking to his disciples in Jn. 16:1 in the context of his pending crucifixion but in the same way, through the entire testimony of the Bible, God has told us everything we need to know, warned us of every snare and bog, shared every possible scenario we might face, in order that we might be prepared.

What's more, God has assured us we will not be alone for He is always with us.

Holy and Eternal God, Give us today your undivided grace. Prepare us for all that you have planned and remind us that you, and you alone, are sovereign. In your mercy, continue the forgiveness you established from the beginning of creation. And, may your love be manifest in our lives today as we love others in your name. AMEN

***

Day 2

God, listen to my cry; pay attention to my prayer! When my heart is weak, I cry out to you from the very ends of the earth. Lead me to the rock that is higher than I am because you have been my refuge, a tower of strength in the face of the enemy. Please let me live in your tent forever! Please let me take refuge in the shelter of your wings!   Ps 61:1-4 (CEB)

Taking time to give attention to the things God has created seems to be more and more challenging, in this age. Too many things seem to scream for our attention. Children, finances, health, work, or unemployment, broken relationship, feelings of failure, the list goes on and on. So many competing factors tend to distract from what is real and genuine, the presence of God Almighty.

When we give God proper position in our lives the distracting issues don't disappear, they simply no longer distract! Why? Because when our attention is focused on

God all issues of distraction are proactively dealt with. Children are safely in the arms of God, even when they set out to experiment in life. When we place God at the head of the line in our finances, referring to tithing, we are blessed by God and the worries subside; "Bring the tithes into the storehouse so there will be enough food in my Temple. If you do," says the Lord of Heaven's Armies, "I will open the windows of heaven for you. I will pour out a blessing so great you won't have enough room to take it in! Try it! Put me to the test!" (Mal 3:10 NLT)

We can apply that verse to every concern we would ever have. If we put God first in our relationships, if we put God first with our children, if we put God first in our work, if we put God first in every single thing we do the result will be consistent. God will "pour out a blessing so great you won't have enough room to take it in!"

Walking with God means acknowledging God is here. Not just in the times of trouble, but in all times. In time of peace and in time of war, in times of joy and in times of sorrow, in times of health and in times of sickness, in times of life and in times of death, God is here!

A blessed day, O God, you have given me. As today signals a new opportunity to trust you and to dwell in your love, give me a special sense of your presence. As the birds sing their songs of praise, the squirrels chatter out their hymns and the gentle breeze testifies to your passing by; you have blessed me with a new and special day. But not for myself only do I pray this day. Heavenly Spirit, as the call of the mourning dove reminds me; please comfort those who mourn and struggle to move on. Give peace and knowledge of eternity, and a bright hope for tomorrow. All of this I pray in Sabbath obedience. AMEN

***

Day 3

Then God spoke all these words: I am the LORD your God who brought you out of Egypt, out of the house of slavery. You must have no other gods before me. Do not make an idol for yourself – of anything in the sky above or on the earth below or in the waters under the earth. Do not bow down to them or worship them, because I, the LORD your God am a passionate God. I punish children for their parent's sins to the third and fourth generations of those who hate me. But I am loyal and gracious to the thousandth generation of those who love me and keep my commandments. Ex 20: 1-6 (CEB)

"Keep your eye on the ball!" How many of us remember a coach, or a parent constantly saying this to us when we were young aspiring baseball stars? The reason they said that is, it is a fundamental requirement for the game. To hit the ball was the object of the game, no hit no run scored. No runs scored meant no winning the game. There is a connection with our Christian faith, the object of the "game" is to worship, adore and praise God. If we fail to make God THE priority of our lives, we fail in worship, adoration and praise!

Worship requires putting God in the fundamental position of number One. When Christians gather the reason for their gathering is God. When Christians sing we sing out of adoration for God. And when Christians pray the intention is to begin with giving thanks to God and praise God for all we have received. Would we really want any other person, or object, to be the recipient of our attention? What shiny new car would listen to our prayers? What bank account would look at our sinful, depraved behavior and have mercy on us? Which of our friends, or family, or coworkers has created the universe and everything in it?

No, God and only God is the rightful recipient of our allegiance. God gives us everything and demands one thing in return; that we put Him first before every other thing in this world. And the result is greater than any home run Babe Ruth, or Roger Maris, or Mickey Mantle every hit, God is "loyal and gracious to the thousandth generation of those who love (Him)".

Dear God, when I am tempted to put my selfish preference before you, I struggle for direction, my life is rudder-less. Direct my every step on this journey of discovery. Show me your will and gently woo me into your presence in Sabbath and reverence. God, today, I pray for your servants seeking direction and knowledge of how best to serve you. In the dark paths of this world, shine your light of confidence and peace. Forgive all sins and make certain a devoted following of your ways. Remind us always of your faithful promise of loyalty and grace, for a thousand generations of those who keep your commandments. AMEN

***

Day 4

For the sin of this one man, Adam, caused death to rule over many. But even greater is God's wonderful grace and his gift of righteousness, for all who receive it will live in triumph over sin and death through this one man, Jesus Christ... So just as sin ruled over all people and brought them to death, now God's wonderful grace rules instead, giving us right standing with God and resulting with eternal life through Jesus Christ our Lord. Rom 5:17,21 (NLT)

In today's world we often think in terms of scarcity, this causes us to conserve and hold back from using what God has given us. This phenomenon also impacts the way we receive the gifts and blessing God offers. We quantify, and inventory, even God's blessings as if there are only a limited number of blessings God will bestow. Sound strange? Well, how many times do we struggle, wrestle, or do battle with major issues in our lives and someone has the audacity to ask: Have you prayed about it and asked God for help? What we have here is an unconscious behavior that shows we are convinced we can either do it ourselves, or that God is too busy to help. GOD IS NEVER TOO BUSY TO HELP!

Grace has been defined as unmerited favor. That is a good way to think of God's grace, we do nothing to earn it, and we certainly don't deserve it in most cases. And God favors each one of us as if we are the only object of this divine love and affection. Grace, however, is even more than that. Grace is a tsunami of God's love.

A tsunami is defined as; "a series of water waves caused by the displacement of a large volume of a body of water" and, in recent years, the world has seen some devastating affect from these unannounced acts of God. Nothing, no one, can escape the impact in a region hit by a tsunami; the water rises and covers everything. Now, our experience of tsunami has been one of tragedy. But even in a water tsunami God's "Grace Tsunami" prevails. You see, just as the rising water covers everything in its path, so too, God's grace covers all creation. Even the most unsuspecting, even the guilty, even the very ones who cause tremendous pain and heartache.

There is no end to the love God has for all of us. In every day of joy, God is there; in every day of sorrow, God is there; in every day of tragedy brought by evil, God is there; and in every instance in which we sin and fall short of the life God has called us to, God is there. So on we go, not alone but covered, submerged, and filled by God's grace.

O God, Welcome to this new day in my life. Your love and forgiveness have replaced my shame. You have reached into the depths of my world and lifted me up. Today, Lord, guide my every step into the presence of your righteousness. Comfort those who struggle with illness or injury. Give peace to those gripped by anxiety, and provide for those who hunger for daily food. Holy Spirit, come into the lives of all of us who need you today. Thank you for the free gift of your grace, I thank you that you do not force me to demonstrate worthiness, or to earn your love. Thank you for being more than I could ever dream of being. In total peace, joy and love for you I pray. AMEN!

***

Day 5

God! My God! It's you—I search for you! My whole being thirsts for you! My body desires you in a dry and tired land, no water anywhere. Yes, I've seen you in the sanctuary; I've seen your power and glory. My lips praise you because your faithful love is better than life itself! Ps 63:1-3 (CEB)

"Prayer – secret, fervent, believing prayer – lies at the root of all personal godliness." William Carey

Many Christian, and pre-Christian, people consider prayer an art, or at the very least a gift that few have mastered. How many times do we ask: Have you prayed about it? Only to hear,: "I don't know how," or, "I'm not comfortable praying." Or, how many times have we heard; "Don't ever ask me to pray in public!"

Our level of comfort is directly related to our intimacy with God. Intimacy is best defined as; "a desire to know and to be known." It is not either or, it is both. I cannot intimately know any person unless I also have a desire to be known, to be open and to share my deepest feelings. When I do so I am placing myself in a vulnerable position, trusting that I will not be taken advantage of and the response is reciprocal.

In the Bible we often read of various "prayer postures" one of which is to fall prostrate before God, surrendered, lying on the ground face down, arms to the side, completely vulnerable and at God's mercy. This is the way ancients would approach a king, and in some cases the king would actually slay the person with the sword out of offense for their audacity to approach, well within the cultural prerogative. So what exactly is prayer is prayer dangerous? No.

Prayer is nothing more than intimate conversation with God, whom we know, and love and desire to be near. Prayer does not need to be eloquent, "O Thou Omnipotent and Holy God of the Universe!" prayer just needs to be real; "God I need you!" Jesus said; "But when you pray, go away by yourself, shut the door behind you, and pray to your Father in private..." (Matt 6:6) by this he meant we are to be intimately connected with God when we pray, even if we are praying in public, our posture must be one of privacy, inviting others into our intimate conversation with God, the One who has loved us, cared for us and forgiven us. How much more intimate can God's love be for us?

God of life, you stand ready to heal and give strength to the weary. Fill me with your peace today. Bring direction into my wandering and reveal your power in my life. I have absolute confidence in your desire to make me whole and I seek only one thing; your will. O God, replace my selfish wishes with your will and make a home within my heart for Your Holy Spirit. Through Christ, who saves me, I pray. AMEN!

***

Day 6

Then I observed that most people are motivated to success because they envy their neighbors. But this, too, is meaningless – like chasing the wind. Fools fold their idle hands, leading them to ruin. And yet, better to have one handful with quietness than two handfuls with hard work and chasing the wind. Ecc 4:4-6 (NLT)

"Who is it that makes muddy water clear? But if allowed to remain still, it will gradually become clear of itself." Tao Te Ching

In this world there are many distractions, noise that fills the ear, sights that grab our attention, worries that occupy our minds and heartbreaks that overwhelm our every thought. If we focus on these alone we are soon adrift in a sea of misguided thoughts and priorities. Now, we know we can do nothing to rid our lives of these things, but there is a way to manage them and our example comes from the exemplary life of Jesus Christ.

Jesus often went away to a quiet place, to a place where the distractions of earthly life could be left behind. The distractions were still there but they were not invited along, if you know what I mean. Even at the moment when Jesus knew he was about to be betrayed and arrested he had perhaps a thousand things on his mind but taking time to be still and pray took precedence. His initial, human, desire was for the whole incident to be over; "please take this cup of suffering away from me." But in the stillness his spirit was calmed and he continued; "Yet I want your will to be done, not mine." (Mk 14:36)

Jesus showed us that we can do the same; after all he was in human form, just as human as he was divine. He was susceptible to heartbreak and worry just like you and me. So we too can intentionally take ourselves away to a quiet place and be alone with God, filtering out all the baggage weighing our spirits down and lifting ourselves up above all the strife and trials. Is it easy? No, just look at the difficulty Peter had staying awake in Mark 14, his physical need for rest overcame his spiritual need for peace. That is why we must focus on God in our quiet time, God's presence in our heart is filling, and God's presence in our mind is filling. When we invite God in there is no room for the worldly things that overwhelm us. It doesn't take a great deal of time, according to Solomon, in Ecclesiastes 4; quietness is twice as valuable as our struggles. I think we can accept that equation any day.

Most precious and loving God of the universe, your invitation to rest is rooted in your wisdom. Your spiritual gravity, designed to make all things settle in my life, gives me peace. Allow my spirit to remain still today, and help me feel a renewed energy and gradual clarity of perception. Help me lie down in green pastures and walk beside still waters as you restore my soul. In Your full and beautiful name, Father, Son and Holy Spirit I pray. AMEN

***

Day 7

If you stop trampling the Sabbath, stop doing whatever you want on my holy day, and consider the Sabbath a delight, sacred to the LORD, honored, and honor it instead of doing things your way, seeking what you want and doing business as usual, then you will take delight in the LORD. I will let you ride on the heights of the earth; I will sustain you with the heritage of your ancestor Jacob. The mouth of the LORD has spoken. Is 58:13-14 (CEB)

We often wonder what we are here, on the earth, for. What is the reason, or the purpose for our existence? Well, the Bible follows a single narrative that speaks of the very reason for our existence. We exist; we were created by God to be loved by God. It's as simple as that we were created as an object of God's love!

Look at the creation account in Genesis and you will see that the entire world, and everything in it, was created by God for the purpose of providing for humankind. The cycles of night and day give proper time to work and to rest. The living creatures on the land, air and water all provide for humanity. Think about it, the medicines developed every day to assist in healing and cures for disease all come from the common elements on, and in, the earth which God created: For what purpose? The purpose of all God's creation is to demonstrate God's unending love for all humanity.

But God's love has been manifest in much greater ways than cure for sickness and disease. God's love has been poured out in the spiritual realm as well. Christ's words in John 3:16 declare a loving and providing God for eternity. "For God so loved the world that he gave his one and only Son. That whosoever would believe in him should not perish but have eternal life!" That is a saying worth dedicating one's life to!

Now, if God has done this for me, I will worship and give absolute prominence to God in my heart. Sabbath is for acknowledging God and setting aside time to do nothing more than that. May God richly bless our times of worship and praise, and may we know that all we see, hear, touch, smell and know is a gift from the Almighty.

This is a new day of living for you, O God. Grant peace that the concerns and worries of this world may be set aside. Make room in my heart for Shabbat, for rest. Give birth within my spirit a place for love, friendship, prayer, touch and singing. Replace the sorrow of my sin with the joy of forgiveness and make the rule of my life the forgiveness of all others. Fill my heart with the assurance of your promise and hope. Now to You, O God, I dedicate this day of living for the sake of the Kingdom of Jesus Christ, AMEN.

***

Day 8

In the beginning God created the heavens and the earth. The earth was formless and empty, and darkness covered the deep waters. And the Spirit of God was hovering over the surface of the waters. Then God said, "Let there be light," and there was light. Gen 1:1-3 (NLT)

17

Life brings us many issues to worry about and all of them are temporary. Why do we spend so much energy on what has so little meaning for eternity? We probably do so because we swim in a sea of temporary existence. No doubt we can all remember a corner of the yard, or the side of a busy street, where there once stood a tall and mighty oak tree, but today that spot is empty, the tree having been cut down for convenience or perhaps due to disease. Or maybe we remember a place where a big red barn stood in the countryside, or a large factory in the city, but now there is an open emptiness in that place. Temporary, each one, and that is the nature of this life. So why do we worry, is it because we think in temporary terms? Do we worry because we know that the things we need to survive are not forever?

Jesus was very clear on the topic of worry, he said; "That is why I tell you not to worry about everyday life – whether you have enough food to eat or enough clothes to wear. For life is more than food, and your body more than clothing. Look at the ravens. They don't plant or harvest or store food in barns, for God feeds them. And you are far more valuable to him than any birds." (Lk 12:22-24 NLT)

Life only brings one valid issue about which we should be concerned and that is eternity. The ironic thing is, when we are concerned about eternity and we make a decision to trust God with our eternal state, all other worry ceases! I don't have any need to be concerned about what I will eat tomorrow if God is the rudder steering my life because I will be living a life of stewardship. Again, another example from nature would be the squirrel, like the birds the squirrel is provided for by God. However, the diet the squirrel lives on is one of seasonal provision so there is the need to gather and store for the barren winter months. The squirrel does work hard to store enough winter food, but I have yet to see a squirrel cowered in the corner racked with worry about what it would eat tomorrow!

It is wise for all of us to allow God to provide, to gather and store, just what we need, and use the rest of our time to glorify His name. Our energy is much better used in helping others know the God we know, the One who provides and the One who loves so much that we will never be in want. No need to worry, God is in control.

Spirit of God, move over me today. In a new beginning, make fresh my awareness of your creation. In my emptiness, fill my heart with promise – pregnant with new direction and passion to serve you. In the rhythm of my life, play a beautiful melody of love upon the strings of my heart and re-create my spirit for your glory; in the name of the Risen Christ. AMEN

***

Day 9

So, brothers and sisters, because of God's mercies, I encourage you to present your bodies as a living sacrifice that is holy and pleasing to God. This is your appropriate priestly service. Don't be conformed to the patterns of this world, but be transformed by the renewing of your minds so that you can figure out what God's will is – what is good and pleasing and mature. Rom 12:1-2 (CEB)

Life is tough: How many times have we either heard, or said that? Well life is tough, and that's a fact, but life is manageable. Every day we have certain tasks we perform without even thinking about them, things like rolling out of bed on the same side each morning. Maybe that's why we say, when someone's having a bad day; "Get out of bed on the wrong side of the bed this morning?" Meaning, the routine was broken and that was the reason for a bad mood. Just think for a moment about what you do every morning without thinking. Have you ever driven to work or school and arrived and suddenly thought: "I don't remember the drive to here!"? The reason is; we have within our brains something called a reticular activating system, or some call it an internal clock. This system is a sort of "auto pilot" program that we develop over time by repeating the same task over and over again. For example, most people set an alarm clock to awaken at the same time every morning and frequently wake up just a minute or so before the alarm goes off. Now, if you set it for a different time, earlier than your regular time, you will probably sleep soundly until the alarm sounds. Here's the thing; waking at the same time every day prepares us to awaken at the same time tomorrow.

What if we were to condition, or program our mind for the purpose of pleasing God in the same way? You see, patterns of the world are similar to our circadian rhythm, that's the fancy name for our internal clock. Sometimes we can become so involved with the daily task of survival that we forget God is with us. We forget to give God first position in our day and invite God to walk with us as we face our challenges. And what is perhaps even more tragic, we lose our connection to God's will for our lives. If this is the case, what are we really committed to?

In the Bible the word commit is used frequently, either in describing sins committed, or being committed to God. In 2 Chronicles 16:9 God spoke through the prophet Hanani to King Asa and said; "The eyes of the LORD search the whole earth in order to strengthen those whose hearts are fully committed to him..." King Asa had become so concerned with his daily life and preserving his earthly position and possessions that he no longer made room for God. Here's the question for the day: Am I too busy to see God today? I hope I am never too busy or occupied with the meaningless thoughts of everyday tasks to acknowledge the One who has given me this life. What's more, I want to develop a regular practice of meeting with God everyday: How about you?

Give me a glimpse of your glory, O God, and a taste of your mercy. Then I shall be renewed by Your Spirit and made whole. Guide me through the challenges of this world that I may be filled with the knowledge of your will and desire what you desire as I serve as you have called me to serve. AMEN.

***

Day 10

Jesus replied, "Now the time has come for the Son of Man to enter into his glory. I tell you the truth, unless a kernel of wheat is planted in the soil and dies, it remains alone. But its death will produce many kernels – a plentiful harvest of new lives. Those who love their life in this world will lose it. Those who care nothing for their life in this world will keep it for eternity." Jn 12:23-25 (NLT)

"If you want to become full, let yourself be empty. If you want to be reborn, let yourself die." Tao Te Ching

Solomon wrote in Ecclesiastes 3, "There is a time for everything under the sun." Yes, there is a time for everything and God is the time keeper, giving order to the world and providing opportunity for us to complete the tasks given us. But what happens when God calls us to do something and we don't respond? Does God give up? Was the task not really necessary? Does God turn away from us and leave us? The answer to each of these questions is clearly no.

Like many people you may have felt a call from God to volunteer, to start something new, or to reach out and help someone who may be struggling only to ignore the feelings in your heart and move on to something else. Did the need go away, or did you simply direct your attention elsewhere? One reason we tend to shy away from these God callings is because we don't really know what is required of us. Well, here's what the Bible says; "...the LORD has told you what is good, and this is what he requires of you: to do what is right, to love mercy, and to walk humbly with your God." (Mic 6:8 NLT)

Doing what is right, loving mercy and walking humbly are three things in direct contrast to behavior which survival in this world seems to call for. Too often the world contradicts what God calls us to, that's why we must experience a change. We must change what and whom we are living for if we want to fulfill God's call.

22

And the more we work to that goal the more influence and impact we will have on the lives around us. Our family, our coworkers, our friends and even the stranger we meet along the way will all be impacted by what we do and say. But the most powerful and noticeable change will be within ourselves. We will look different, we will speak differently, we will be found in different surroundings, we will begin leading rather than following and we will find ourselves in the presence of God wherever we go. How can that not be where we belong and where we desire to be?

Father in heaven, give me quiet in the midst of a noisy world so I may hear you. Give me rest within my soul so I may know you. Above all else, give me release from this world so I may be born anew in the freshness of your love. Fill my empty spirit with Your Holy Spirit and give me a fresh understanding of your love for all your children. AMEN.

***

Day 11

There's a season for everything and a time for every matter under the heavens:...a time for tearing and a time for repairing, a time for keeping silent and a time for speaking, Eccl 3:1,7 (CEB)

"It is easier to be silent altogether than to speak with moderation." Thomas a Kempis

God has created a world that is filled with His presence. Even when we go to the most remote places, God is there. Even when we think we are completely alone, God is there. For example: there is only one true silent place and that is within a sound proof booth used by doctors to test one's hearing. And still there is the sound of breath rhythmically rushing in and out of the lungs; God is there. Once, when astronaut John Glen was in the space capsule, in the absolute silence of space, he was awakened from a deep sleep by a strange noise. He could hear a "wooshing" sound, as he described it. Later it was determined that the sound he heard, ironically in absolute silence, was the blood pumping through his arteries. And God was there!

How often we think God has left us and we stand on our own, but as someone once said, that is when God is most near. You see, in this life there are many distracting issues and experiences that cause us to focus on the wrong things. My immediate need, according to my will, is to temporarily preserve my comfort, my ease, myself. However, my true need, according to God's will, is nothing more than to praise and follow God and in following God I will preserve my comfort, my ease, myself eternally!

Jesus said, "The harvesters are paid good wages, and the fruit they harvest is people brought to eternal life. What joy awaits both the planter and the harvester alike!" (Jn 4:36) meaning the more we acknowledge the presence and the sovereignty of God, the greater we will be blessed. The more I put God in the place He deserves, first place, the result is more of God and less of me! The more I silence self and the world around me the more I hear from God! So now today, this very moment, let's be silent and listen for the voice of God in the breeze, the birds, the very beating of our hearts. Yes, God is here!

God of the universe, provide me today with open eyes and a closed mouth. Silence my thoughts of angst and concern and fill me with knowledge of your peace. Calm my heart and fill my ears with your sweet messages of love, joy, peace and forgiveness. For those with whom I journey through this world, give them peace today and the assurance of your unfailing love. In the name of the Risen Christ: AMEN.

***

Day 12

Don't do anything for selfish purposes, but with humility think of others as better than yourselves. Instead of each person watching out for their own good, watch out for what is better for others. Adopt the attitude that was in Christ Jesus: Phil 2:3-5 (CEB)

"As Thou wilt; what Thou wilt; when Thou wilt." Thomas a Kempis

As difficult as this may be to accept, the world does not revolve around me! Coming to that conclusion one soon realizes that there are still many people who believe the world does revolve around them, and they view every experience from the perspective of gain verses loss. Not gains and loss for the Kingdom of God but for themselves, and ironically even Kingdom issues become classified as net gains and net losses by many Christians demonstrating how deeply we are affected by our human condition. Believe it or not, God is not concerned with our net gains or losses; God is focused on our gross gains and losses!

John Wesley once asked, "Are the things you are doing bearing fruit?" This simple question is focused on the real issue. You see, there are certain factors in the Kingdom of God that we can do nothing about and the greatest of these is the behavior of other people. Yes, when it comes to behavior we have influence on only one person, ourselves! So, in the process of sharing our faith and adding to the Kingdom of God there will be regular losses, but if we fail to press on for the gains we are not fulfilling God's call, we are not bearing fruit. You see, God said in the creation narrative, "Be fruitful and multiply." Nowhere did God say take an inventory, or always show a profit. Quite the contrary, Christians are called to give all with no consideration to the issue of profit, especially personal profits.

So, what are we to make of all this? It's simple, trust God. Trusting in God means allowing God's will to be done, and God's will is that each of us would be faithful in the process of sharing God's love with others, then it is up to them to make a decision. When we are faithful we continue sharing, not stopping to take inventory, or put notches on our belts representing our conquests, we move on and continue to share God's love. What a wonderful world this will be when we all focus on God's will, not ours.

Dear Lord, turn my heart away from selfish desires and toward you today. Father, Son and Holy Spirit fill me with your goodness, and guide me into greater heights of obedience to you. Enfold me with your love through Your Word and lead me to a better relationship with you and those who travel by my side. Grant me your forgiveness and make me an instrument of your peace, an ambassador for You. AMEN.

***

Day 13

The LORD is my shepherd. I lack nothing. He lets me rest in grassy meadows; he leads me to restful waters; he keeps me alive. He guides me in proper paths for the sake of his good name. Ps 23:1-3 (CEB)

When going on a trip or vacation we always find it wise to plan our travels. The first step is to decide on our destination and how long we will be there. The second step may be to look at a map and plan the proper driving route. Do we want to drive on the freeway or would we rather take the back roads? Or, maybe we will be using one of the Airlines to get us where we're going, so we either visit a Travel Agent, or we use our computer and find the best possible deal online. Then we need to plan our activities while we are there: What will we do each day? Are there sightseeing excursions we will want to experience? What sort of entertainment will we enjoy? Are there relatives in the area we will need to visit? Many things need to be decided before the trip begins but many times the last decision is the most difficult, after all the planning and the exciting anticipation of the trip we need to decide how much it will cost!

Well, there is one trip we can plan in a similar way. The destination is the most beautiful, peaceful, joyful, and entertaining and fun we will ever experience, it is literally out of this world! The transportation is the most efficient we will ever experience such that the greatest and fastest airplane could never match. Every day will be filled with excitement and joy and the best part of the whole trip is this; we don't have to pay for it! We simply have to decide to go! Imagine a place where there is no end to happiness, no concerns about how tomorrow will be. Imagine a place where there is an endless supply of everything you need. Imagine a place where everyone treats you as if they have known you forever, a place where you will never feel pain, where you will shed only tears of joy!

Where exactly is this place and why doesn't everyone want to go there? Well, I can't tell you exactly where it is because I don't know the location but I do know we call this place Heaven and Heaven is where God is! In fact, God has a paid in full ticket for anyone who would like to go, paid in full with the blood of Jesus Christ. You see, sin cannot be present in Heaven and that's why God took care of paying the price to absolve all sin past, present and future. The reason God went to such extremes is because God wants everyone to be in Heaven where all we would ever need or want will be, forever and ever. The question is: Are we all aboard? Because God will not take us there unwillingly, we must say yes!

Where is the line to board? Well it's right here in this earth. We serve God every day of our life and we take one more step in the line before God decides the eternal trip begins. So, get in line and stay in line, that's my plan!

Precious Lord, take my hand as you lead me through this Promised Land! May my heart be filled with the knowledge of this life lived for you, and may my day be a day lived in complete obedience to your call. O God, reveal the mystery of forgiveness to me, show me how wonderful life is when lived with you. May your blessing fall upon all your servants today and may all see the joy of this life, in all circumstances. This I pray, through the loving heart and life of Jesus Christ. AMEN

***

Day 14

Be still and know that I am God! I will be honored by every nation. I will be honored throughout the world. The LORD of heaven's Armies is here among us; the God of Israel is our fortress. Ps 46:10-11 (NLT)

"When you realize there is nothing lacking, the whole world belongs to you" Lao-Tzu

There's a great old hymn; "He's Got the Whole World in His Hands", that I remember learning as a child in Mrs. Graham's Children's Choir. Everything in this world is held together by God, everything is touched by God, everything is impacted by God, EVERYTHING! And God has given it all to you and me to use and care for. But too often we function as if God is not involved. Oh yes, things happen to us as if God was not with us, but the reality is that is when God is closest to us. In triumph as in tragedy, God walks by our side.

Jesus said, "I have told you all this that you may have peace in me. Here on earth you will have many trials and sorrows. But take heart, because I have overcome the world." (Jn 16:33) We need to give attention to how Jesus overcame. Did he do it by himself? Did Jesus have some sort of self-help book he

29

read? Did Jesus have powerful and influential friends who helped him? The answer is no to all, and any other possibility except one. The One who enabled Jesus to overcome happened to be his Heavenly Father, God. God provides the strength to win, the mind to know, and the heart to persevere. Yes, God does indeed have the whole world in His hands. Aren't you glad?

Holy God, as I exhale the worries and concerns of the world, may all that I inhale fill my life with your goodness. You have provided all I need; there is no cause to wait upon you. You have impregnated the whole world with potential for this new day. So, now I surrender and lift up my eyes to see your magnificent glory and to acknowledge your sovereign majesty. Speak your words of assurance to me, once again, that I may hear and respond to you. Bless all who worship you this day as preparation for complete Sabbath rest. AMEN.

***

Day 15

God says, "Because you are devoted to me, I'll rescue you. I'll protect you because you know my name. Whenever you cry out to me, I'll answer. I'll be with you in troubled times. I'll save you and glorify you." Ps 91:14-15 (CEB)

"Only listen to the voices of pines and cedars, when no wind stirs." Ryo-Nen

Looking for God seems to be one of the most prevalent activities for people struggling with life challenges, especially in times of abrupt change. Changes can cause our minds to wonder about God's existence, for example, a diagnosis of cancer, the death of a loved one, the prospect of a new job or the loss of a current job, difficulty with a son or daughter, or even the observation of a family member experiencing a difficult change in their life. All these, and many more, instances in life often cause us to wonder: Is God real? And when we wonder we search, we seek, we investigate. Some may even travel to solitary places in which to meditate and pray, or if unsure they may just go away to think.

When Isaiah found his life in turmoil he cried out to God, complaining that the people would not listen to him. In a way God's point to Elijah was; they don't listen because they are hearing the wrong voice! So God sends Elijah to the mountain and says: "Go out and stand before me on the mountain. And as Elijah stood there, the LORD passed by, and a mighty windstorm hit the mountain. It was such a terrible blast that the rocks were torn loose, but the LORD was not in the wind. After the wind there was an earthquake. And after the earthquake there was a fire, but the LORD was not in the fire. And after the fire there was the sound of a gently whisper." (1 Kgs 19:11-12)

Elijah was expecting to hear something bold and undeniable, a loud and commanding voice but instead he heard a gentle whisper. Maybe, when we feel the need to search for God, we should just take some time and listen to the many ways God is speaking to us, not in loud profound noise but in simple and calm messages brought to us in the morning breeze or the gentle rains. Listen, do you hear God?

31

To you, O God, I call out for healing and deliverance from the limitations of this mortal body. In sickness I am made whole, in poor health I am made strong, and in sin I am made clean by your mighty hand. Make straight the path to my heart, for the goodness of your presence, O LORD. AMEN.

***

Day 16

Everything is wearisome beyond description. No matter how much we see, we are never satisfied. No matter how much we hear, we are not content. History repeats itself. It has all been done before. Nothing under the sun is truly new. Eccl 1:8-9 (NLT)

Each day there are many people in this world who struggle for survival. We don't often consider the suffering of others because we feel challenged in our own life, that's why millions starve and go without a roof over their heads while we Americans worry about affording a vacation this year. Our vision is hobbled by our personal situation. Now, there is nothing wrong with a concern for personal wellbeing, after all, God wants to bless us. But I think what God really wants is for us to find that blessing in helping others.

Time and time again people who help others experience more of a blessing than those who were helped. Several years ago we went to Durango Mexico and worked with a local church called Casa D'Vita Passe, a new church start filled with middle class young people. The church had a unique vision of building a house of worship and moving out of the tire warehouse they had been using. But they were not building among the middle class homes in the area; they chose to build their church among the poor and destitute outside the city, people living in slab wood shacks with dirt floors.

One evening we had a fiesta, a party at which we grilled hamburgers at the new building site and invited the neighborhood. As the people lined up they loaded their arms with food but one little boy caught my attention. I remembered him from the Bible School we were offering each morning, his name was Poncho. Poncho came through the line multiple times, each time he would run away behind the building only to return a few minutes later. After his third time through I followed him to see what he was doing. He was stashing the food behind the walls of a one room home that was in process of construction and not yet finished. I was careful not to let him see me so he wouldn't feel he was in trouble.

When I returned to the fiesta I asked Juan, our host, what he thought Poncho was doing. He told me that Poncho, who was nine years old, was getting food for his family. He had a mother and 4 sisters at home and he, Poncho, at nine years old, was their only provider since his father went into the mountains looking for gold and never returned. Suddenly I realized that this small boy was forced to become an adult and provider for an entire family. To me this was unusual, but to Poncho and many others like him this is life. Now, I was blessed by Poncho because from that day on I know my wellbeing depends on my service to God, not on what I have.

Dear Lord, open my eyes to your love today. Help my mind find rest from the concerns of life, and take refuge only in you. Give me a satisfied heart today, O God, and make my spirit right with yours. God, please give to those in need, and bring relief to all those who are sick and injured in any way. Give peace to the confused and strength to the abused. Through Jesus Christ our Lord I pray. AMEN

***

Day 17

I thank you for answering my prayer and giving me victory! The stone that the builders rejected has now become the cornerstone. This is the LORD'S doing, and it is wonderful to see. This is the day the LORD has made. We will rejoice and be glad in it. Ps 118:21-24 (NLT)

The dawn of a new day: What will we experience, what will we be challenged by, what will bring us joy or sorrow today? Perhaps something left over from yesterday still weighs heavy on the mind, or maybe there is concern for an upcoming event we know we are not prepared to face. What does this new day bring to us?

Jesus, in preparing his disciples for a life of ministry, always focused on the value of individual commitment as a means to affect the community, and beyond. For example, read the Beatitudes from the Sermon on the Mount given to us in Matthew 5. In the first twelve verses Jesus gives no less than nine opportunities for blessing. The first of which is basic and fundamental to our faith; "God blesses those who are poor and realize their need for him, for the Kingdom of Heaven is theirs." (Matt. 5:3 NLT) Realizing our need for God is not always our reaction when we find ourselves in need, but Jesus' point here to his disciples is simply this; God provides what we need and if we fail to acknowledge God we will not experience the blessing and we will fail to see what God provides.

We all know that with a little effort, and perhaps some good fortune, we can provide for ourselves and meet our needs for this new day. We can find ways to survive, humanity has been doing that forever. Survival breeds innovation and innovation makes a way. However, there is one very important fact to remember when we provide for ourselves. Our provision is temporary and the day will surely come when we are no longer able to accomplish what we need. God, on the other hand, provides for us eternally and when we know we need God that is when we are blessed by God. When we know we need God we know that today's challenge has been met, we know that tomorrow is securely in God's hands. So, for us to be blessed all God requires of us today is to know we need Him!

Today, O Lord, I build my Ebenezer, an altar on which I place all things most dear to me. My wife, family, my church, my ministry and my life; I give back to you. I release the need to hold on, and I give completely to you, knowing these things rightfully belong to you from the beginning. I thank you, God, for the gift these are to me and I accept the responsibility of stewardship for each of them. May your blessing be upon all that is yours, today and forever: AMEN!

Day 18

Who among you by worrying can add a single moment to your life? And why do you worry about your clothes? Notice how the lilies of the field grow. They don't wear themselves out with work, they don't spin cloth. But I say to you that even Solomon in all his splendor wasn't dressed like one of these. If God dresses the grass of the field so beautifully, even though it's alive today and tomorrow it's thrown into the furnace, won't God do much more for you, you people of weak faith? Matt 6:27-30 (CEB)

"It is useful during Sabbath to clarify or reaffirm those principles that calibrate our inner compass to illuminate our inner direction" Wendell Berry

In business the inventory, or audit, is most important. The amount of product available in the warehouse on January 1, and its value, versus the same number on December 31 is the chief indicator of the wellbeing of that business. A healthy business is one which shows a profit, or at least avoids a loss. How often do we conduct our lives in a similar manner? And then again, can our lives be measured for effectiveness based on our profit margin? I really think if we always consider the profitability of daily life we would be in very bad condition indeed.

Where would the Christian church be today if people like Barnabas decided the city of Antioch was not worth his time? Barnabas went to Antioch because he had heard of the people there who had fled Jerusalem and began sharing the ways of Jesus with the Hellenistic

36

Jewish residents. The Hellenists were heavily influenced by the Greek Wisdom of the time and a message about a Savior, who was killed, was not going to be an easy sell, no profit there! And to also try and convince these people, steeped in worldly wisdom that this same Savior arose from the dead, well we're talking a negative profit there for sure. But the people were faithful, even against such odds and Barnabas followed their example. "When he arrived and saw evidence of God's grace, he was overjoyed and encouraged everyone to remain fully committed to the Lord." (Acts 11:23 CEB)

Barnabas saw people helping each other, and helping others come to know the love of Christ. They did not appear to be preaching the message in words; they were preaching the message in action. This so impressed Barnabas that he brought Saul, later named Paul, to Antioch to help him preach and teach the Word. It was here, in Antioch that the name Christian was first used meaning; "follower of Christ". All because a group of people refused to live their lives based on what was in it for them; they lived based on their knowledge of God whom they knew would take care of them. When we follow that example our inventory is overflowing and our true, heavenly, profit is uncountable!

LORD of heaven, today I stop counting the things that have no true value. Help me instead to place the greatest value on life lived for you. Show me the riches of laughter and friendship. I am wealthy, rich beyond counting when I take account of family, love and acceptance. And most important of all, I am blessed with the priceless possession of your loving forgiveness through Jesus Christ my Lord. With that I pray for the healing and strength of your people, the Church, from disease and sickness that the hope of salvation may be obtained; in the name of the Father, the Son, and the Holy Spirit. AMEN

***

Day 19

So be truly glad. There is wonderful joy ahead, even though you have to endure trials for a little while. These trials show that your faith is genuine. It is being tested as fire tests and purifies gold – though your faith is far more precious than mere gold. So when your faith remains strong through many trials, it will bring you much praise and glory and honor on the day when Jesus Christ is revealed to the whole world. 1 Pt 1:6-7 (NLT)

"There were times when I could not afford to sacrifice the bloom on the moment to any work, whether of head or hands. They were not times subtracted from my life, but so much over and above my usual allowance." Henry David Thoreah

Given all that God does for me, I am often remiss and fail to acknowledge that all I have and all I am is a gift from God. Morning by morning a new beginning, a blank page, is given me. What will I do with this new day? What portrait shall I paint? What sights will I see? Or: What danger lurks in this day ahead?

No matter the danger, no matter the challenge, for the believer it is onward in Christ's name. As the actor John Wayne once said; "Courage is being scared to death and saddling up anyway!" With Christ, my companion, what have I to fear? Fear is associated with the unknown, when we find ourselves in a dark room we proceed very carefully for fear of tripping or stumbling because we don't know what is in our way. Each new day may begin, for some, in fear not knowing what is ahead. Life itself may be a fearful experience when we focus on the unknown, or when changes come such as the death of a spouse and we don't know what the future holds.

Every Christian finds comfort and security in the knowledge that God is always with us. We may look around and see emptiness, but we know the Spirit of God is always present. You see, when Jesus issues the Great Commission, in Matthew 28, his closing words were; "And remember, I am with you always." (Matt 28:20) Tell me, what evidence do we have that Jesus has not kept that promise? He is with us even when we are not looking for him, he is with us even when we are running from him, and he is with us even when we are sleeping. What will I do today to show my gratitude to God for always being with me? Stay tuned, for I shall begin by thanking God for family, friends, and new acquaintances and then saddle up for the ride for there is wonderful joy ahead!

Holy and loving God, today I seek opportunity for a proper marriage between Sabbath and life. I pray you allow the precious things to be honored in my life – courage, creativity, wisdom, peace, kindness, and delight. May these grow, today, in the soil of all time! May all who love you experience your complete love and presence this day! In Christ I pray. AMEN

***

Day 20

Ask, and you will receive. Search, and you will find. Knock, and the door will be opened to you. For everyone who asks, receives. Whoever seeks, finds. And to everyone who knocks, the door is opened. Matt 7:7-8 (CEB)

"Just to be is a blessing. Just to live is holy." Rabbi Abraham Heschel

What do you want to be, when you grow up? That's the question we were all asked, when we were young. And it's the question we frequently ask children once we have grown up. But sometimes it takes most of a lifetime to figure out what we really want to be. For example; Ghandi was 50 years old when he discovered his desire to live a life in nonviolent resistance. Cervantes was older than that when he began his career as a novelist, and what about Grandma Moses, Colonel Sanders and Dave Thomas! The fact is, God is always working in our lives and just like choosing a lifetime mission, our spiritual mission in life comes when we realize what we are passionate about.

Too many people are unhappy, feeling they are bogged down by the routine daily tasks they must perform in order to survive in this world. You get up in the morning, eat the same breakfast as yesterday, follow the same ritual in waking yourself up, get ready for work, drive or walk the same route to work, sit at the same desk, shuffle the same papers, see the same people, eat the same lunch, accomplish the same minimal requirements to satisfy the boss, drive home, eat dinner, watch some television, and go to bed. Then, the next day you repeat it all over again. What's missing in this picture? Passion!

Passion has been described as something you really love to do. So, what do you really love to do? Then do it for Christ! Do you love to draw? Then do it and teach others, maybe children, how to draw pictures that tell the Gospel story. Do you love to do wood working? Then do it and teach others how to make Christian symbols like crosses etc. You get the picture, now do it. And if you are concerned with the affordability, how you will pay for this new found life, just remember this simple equation; limited resources + passion = innovation! Just do it!

Dear Jesus, as this worldly life continues to serve a steady diet of disappointment. As happiness appears distant, remind me today of what is true so that I do not turn to what is of no real value. Help me taste what has been given to me, take delight in what I already have and see that it is good. Help me focus less on my lack and more on my abundance, which is your love and forgiveness. And may your full blessing rest upon all those whom you have given me to love! I praise you today, my Creator and friend. AMEN

***

Day 21

"You can enter God's Kingdom only through the narrow gate. The highway to hell is broad, and its gate is wide for the many who choose that way. But the gateway to life is very narrow and the road is difficult, and only a few ever find it." Matt 7:13-14 (NLT)

"Let me be employed for thee or laid aside for thee, exalted for thee or brought low for thee." John Wesley

In growing up, we all remember certain things our parents told us. When I was young my father was also my boss as I worked for him in his business building homes. He would always say; "Always be doing something on the job, even if you don't know how to do it, do something!" He would also say; "Doing something right is easier than doing it wrong, because if you do it wrong you will have to fix it!"

So what did I learn from these two statements? One might see them as conflicting messages, polar opposites, seeming to say do but don't do. However, I learned to know them as complimenting statements. You see, these statements were, and are, a call to stewardship. If I am to focus on my task of always doing something, and doing it right, then I must strive to learn exactly how to do it! The result is a feeling of accomplishment and at the end of every day, the knowledge of a job well done.

Living for Christ is exactly the same thing as doing something diligently, and correctly. As we aim for the narrow, and avoid the easiness of the wide road, we come to know the reward of obedience. This reward s not a monetary reward, it's not even an encouraging word. This reward is the peace of mind that comes with knowing we are within the will of Almighty God. So, with respect to every step in life; do something and do it right. You'll be glad you took the time and effort.

God of wind, rain and the calm; remind me, in every moment of this day, how secure I am in your care. Help me grasp the certain hope that comes in taking stock of what you have given me. Give me peace with what I have, and remove my human desire to covet things I have not. In the happiness you give me the wheels of want will grind to a halt, and I shall bask in the glory of all you have blessed me with as I give you thanks for family and work, and recreation. May my life reflect your presence today, AMEN!

* * *

Day 22

All praise to God, the Father of our Lord Jesus Christ, who has blessed us with every spiritual blessing in the heavenly realms because we are united with Christ. Even before he created the world, God loved us and chose us in Christ to be holy and without fault in his eyes. Eph. 1:3-4 (NLT)

Jesus often went away, to a quiet place, for prayer. Prayer is our most effective way to connect with God, and in prayer we also have opportunity to reflect on our personal life. Think of prayer as storytelling, stay with me now, telling God the story of our lives. It's like writing a postcard each day of a vacation, but instead of a "wish you were here" at the close, we articulate a more profound statement. The closing statement on a prayer postcard is more of a "thanks for being here!" declaration.

But many times we find ourselves empty, unable to offer even a postcard type prayer up to God. Well, there's an old story about a three year old girl who had wandered away from her back yard while her mother was hanging laundry on the clothes line. When she was discovered missing her mother was understandably frantic. The vast countryside around their home included hundreds of acres of woods, and literally thousands of acres of farmland. The community responded with every available police officer and many neighbors combing the woods and fields. The parents and close friends of the family were beginning to think the worst as the day drew closer to darkness. Within a couple miles of the little girls home there was a farm, and around dusk, while the Farmer was walking toward the barn, to do his evening chores, he heard something in the distance. He stopped to listen. It was a child singing, the tune was familiar, he remembered his own children singing it when they were young. "ABCDEFG, HIJKLMNOP....." it was the Alphabet Song, the one that most every child learns to sing. Well, the Farmer followed the sound into his cornfield, behind his house. And there, sitting on the ground, he found the missing child.

She looked at him and smiled as she said; "I knew someone would find me! I was praying for you to come."

"What do you mean, praying, I heard you singing the Alphabet Song, not praying."

"Oh", the child said, "I didn't know how to pray, so I decided to sing the Alphabet Song and let Jesus put the words together!"

How about it, why not let Jesus put the words together today, for your postcard prayer? May our spirits find rest and refreshment in knowing God is always by our side, even when we don't know what we should say!

Precious Lord, Your guidance and companionship is all I need for this day. May your shining face be the light by which I navigate through the pitfalls, and the obstacles before me! Your blessings for family, health and wholeness are all I need to succeed in this failure ridden world. And may your blessing and peace be upon all your children as well. In the name of the Risen Christ I pray. AMEN.

***

Day 23

Oh, the joys of those who do not follow the advice of the wicked, or stand around with sinners, or join with the mockers. But they delight in the law of the LORD, meditating on it day and night. They are like trees planted along the river bank, bearing fruit in each season. Their leaves never wither, and they prosper in all they do. Ps 1:1-3 (NLT)

We are faced with many questions, every day and sometimes every hour. Decisions are made regularly and when these decisions are made the impact is spread over many people, not just us. This is called conflict, anytime a decision must be made there is conflict and it starts between the action decided on and the possibility of doing nothing. For some, doing nothing is not an option and this may lead to even more conflict. Maybe you're like this, maybe you have heard someone say; "Why can't you just let it go!"

For the Christian life doing nothing is never an option. We are called to be a part of the solution rather than making a bigger problem by doing nothing. Consider Jesus' story about sowing seeds; we usually focus on the soils in which the seed falls. "As he scattered them across his field, some fell on a footpath, and the birds came and ate them." (Matt 13:4 NLT) Yes, the various types of soil, or ground, on which the seeds were sown have a relevant meaning for us. To prove this point Jesus later explained the soils as representative of what happens after hearing the message, but beyond the soil lies a message about the farmer, the one sowing the seeds.

Jesus said; "Now listen to the explanation of the parable about the farmer planting seeds." (Matt 13:18 NLT) The parable is about the farmer! The farmer could very well have made his decision earlier NOT to go to the field. But thank God he chose to go. The farmer could have made the decision to only sow the seeds in one type of soil; instead he chose to scatter the seeds on all types of soil thus increasing his chances of a good harvest. You see, when we choose to follow where God leads we will soon learn that God takes us even to the places we think we are not welcome or needed. Friend, God is everywhere and calls us to follow. So bear fruit in every season, not just in the easy ones!

Heavenly Father; today I seek a quiet patch of ground in which to grow. A Place surrounded by the protective hedge of your love and affection, even in this busy life. Allow my mind to find rest and comfort in contemplation and meditation on Your Word. Refresh my spirit with your forgiveness and prepare me to serve you, in all you call me to. Rest your full and complete blessing on the hearts of those near me, as well as those I have yet to encounter, and may every step I take, today and every day, bring me closer to your will. In Christ I pray. AMEN.

Day 24

God called him out of the bush, "Moses, Moses!" Moses said, "I'm here." Then the LORD said, "Don't come any closer! Take off your sandals, because you are standing on holy ground." Ex 3:4-5 (CEB)

"Whenever we take off our shoes, we realize we are standing on holy ground." Brother David Steindl-Rast

In the early 1940's there was a basketball coach in Coldwater Michigan name Floyd Eby. Coach Eby was a science teacher in the high school and he also coached the varsity basketball team. Coach Eby was credited with developing the Two Handed Set Shot that revolutionized the game of basketball. But there is a much more notable part of the Coach's life. He was also a staunch atheist which, in that day, was not an easy position to take.

One day, after enduring yet another attempt by his family to convert him, the coach set out to prove God was no more than myth. So, being a science teacher, he decided to prove the nonexistence of God by disproving the concept of creation, scientifically. Over and over again the scientific method was unable to prove any alternative theory of the origin of the universe. As the Coach said; "Everything I tried ended up in the same place." You see, he found that every theory of origin eventually called for a certain level of faith that it was correct. For example; the Big Bang Theory eventually requires faith that a cataclysmic explosion happened and the result was that every minuet, microscopic, mathematical alignment literally fell into place by sheer coincidence in order to bring life into the world, and sustain it.

When Coach Eby realized this he suddenly felt something he had never felt before, he felt a presence of God! He describes a night at his desk that started with a feverish, last ditch, attempt to prove God does not exist, and suddenly he knew, he did not think, he knew without a shadow of a doubt that God does exist and God loved him! Was there a scientific explanation that God does not exist? No! Was there scientific proof that God does exist? Yes, the Coach would tell us, "Look around you, God, my Father in Heaven, owns the whole universe, and everything in it and you can't prove that He doesn't!"

You see, when the same level of faith is applied to the existence of God as one would need to apply to any other theory of origin, God is proven! Have faith and know that God is real, every relationship you have is a product of God's relationship with you. Everything in this world is a result of God who loves you and has created the world to sustain your life. Every person you love, and who loves you, is a result of God's love.

Loving Savior; help me today, that I may feel the tenderness of your presence, through the touch of holy ground. May every step I take provide a tender meeting of body and grass, dirt, sand and rock, and may my steps always be a reminder of your creation and fill my heart with your love. As you have so carefully created and loved the earth, so too, you created and love me. Walk with me, Loving God, and I shall be blessed. AMEN.

***

48

Day 25

Let all that I am praise the LORD; with my whole heart, I will praise his holy name. Let all that I am praise the LORD; may I never forget the good things he does for me. He forgives my sins and heals my diseases. Ps 103:1-3 (NLT)

"The art of medicine consists of amusing the patient while nature cures the disease." Voltaire

Taking life for granted is a very real danger, one that everyone falls into. For example, what thought do we give to the air we breathe? Every life giving breath is more than just something that happens. Hundreds of muscles in our body combine efforts to make our diaphragm move up and down as the air rushes in our lungs. And then consider all the functions of that air. It takes a medical doctor to explain each and every intricate step of the process. Complicated? Yes. But from God's perspective there is but one purpose to it all, to give life!

Just like all the complicated, interconnected, muscles and functions of the human body, we are also connected in community. We need each other, we depend on each other and, ironically, we function better as an individual when we have community connections. For example; in southern Africa there is a tiny, landlocked, country called Lesotho. In Lesotho a man named Larry Pray, (great name) interviewed some of the people as part of his research for a book he was writing titled; Leading Causes of Life.

He asked; "What are your religious health assets in Lesotho?" Answers were: "The mountains, because

49

they are a source of water, a place of safety, and symbols of things that do not change. Then they said: The Rivers and the roads that bring us together, to visit relatives and friends which bring goods to us. We call this Bophelo!"

Bophelo is a word that has a very broad meaning. It means, in short, connected. For the people of Lesotho, being connected, or interdependent, is crucial to their survival. Life is this way for you and me as well. Without all the conscious, and unconscious, functions of community we would not survive. Conflict would be the end of our human community! Perhaps that's why, when God created the world, He created ecosystems and relationships, and community spirit in every living creature and thing. We call it nature, God calls it love!

Dear God, today I ask for the special blessing of finding rest in your love as my heart is healed of all worldly concern. I pray for intimate companionship, seeing, touching and simply being with you. To rest with you, to eat, walk and play with you, for you are my friend and companion through all of life. I ask you to make your blessing known to all I love, to family, friends and associates, so they too may know the endless joy of your love and forgiveness. In Jesus' name I pray. AMEN.

***

Day 26

You are the light of the world. A city on top of a hill can't be hidden. Neither do people light a lamp and put it under a basket. Instead, they put it on top of a lamp stand, and it shines on all who are in the house. In the same way, let your light shine before people, so they can see the good things you do and praise your Father who is in heaven. Matt 5:14-16 (CEB)

"Do you have the patience to wait until the mud settles and the water is clear?" Tao Te Ching

Jesus Christ brought a message into this world that appeared to be antithetical to everything known to humanity. His message seemed to turn everything upside down, no wonder the religious leaders of the time were so upset with him. But it wasn't always that way, Jesus' ministry, which most believe lasted about three years, progressed in three stages; obscurity, popularity, and opposition.

In the first year of his ministry, no one knew who Jesus was so it was natural curiosity that drew the crowds to him. The area in which he traveled was relatively small, about half the size of the state of Michigan, so it was very likely that within every group of people he came in contact with, there would be someone who was related to folks in the next town, or village. So the news would precede him and people would be waiting to hear his message and find healing for every disease and condition they had. Who was he? Was he the Messiah expected to come? Was he going to restore the throne of Israel? They didn't know, or consider these; in the first year of his ministry healing was the primary need for them.

This led to the second year, the year of popularity. It was during this year that Jesus frequently told those he healed; "Tell no one..." Many refer to this as the Messianic Secret, probably for the purpose of avoiding the inevitable conflicts with the Jewish hierarchy. During this year people did more than wait for him in the next venue, they ran to him. Synagogues, homes, and open fields in the countryside filled up with people longing to see, hear and touch him. And thus the year of opposition soon followed. The reason for this was because that which he was teaching involved a personal relationship with God, not a corporate relationship. If people could connect with God, one on one, they would not need the leaders to do it for them and that had become an industry of sorts.

Ironically, Jesus was most effective in the third year, the year of opposition. It was during that year that his teaching was bold and the most enlightening to his disciples. It was during that year that people like Peter began to feel confident enough to express their opinion; Peter and some of the other disciples even began some of their own ministries. All because Jesus had shown them the organic nature of their spiritual existence, in short, they were growing!

So the question for the day is this: Where are you growing?

God of the universe; Reveal to me the hidden wholeness that is present in my soul. Under gird my courage and vision for following you, throughout this day, that my faith may continue to burn bright and hot. I know there is a spark of divine fire within my spirit that refuses to be extinguished, so give me the gift of patience and I shall see the wonderful talents and strengths you have created within me. In Christ I pray. AMEN

***

Day 27

Then the devil took him up and revealed to him all the kingdoms of the world in a moment of time. "I will give you the glory of these kingdoms and authority over them," the devil said, "Because they are mine to give to anyone I please. I will give it all to you if you will worship me." Jesus replied, "The Scriptures say, 'You must worship the LORD your God and serve him only." Lk 4:5-8 (NLT)

"Act as if everything depended on you; trust as if everything depended on God." St. Ignatius

In this life we are conditioned to live as though everything that happens is directly related to behavior, either ours or others. The Jewish laws of retribution were developed to provide punishment for actions deemed to be against God's will. The challenge is in how we determine Gods will! In the Bible we read of many instances where God speaks through prophets, they are the 'thus says the LORD' statements that usually come along when behavior is counter to God's will. That's why most prophets didn't live long lives; they always seemed to tell the people they were doing something wrong. But if retribution, or repayment, for the things people do wrong really worked one would think we would soon see some positive results. Let there be no doubt, behavior that works against God's will has negative consequences but paying back a wrong for a wrong never produces the outcome we desire.

God created humanity as an object of His love and as a result, God has given us what we describe as freewill. God loves us so much; God will never interfere with our freewill. Freewill is the reason so many bad things happen in this world. Enter Satan and temptation of the human desire, corrupted by sin, leads to many misdeeds. That is why Jesus, knowing Satan better than all of us, fashioned his teaching in the positive. The Beatitudes of Matthew 5, in the Sermon on the Mount, are prime examples of positive teaching. "You are blessed…" Jesus begins each one, "when…" showing us that positive behavior is what staves off the Evil One. Allowing the natural consequences to do the teaching in every instance, even when it appears someone is rewarded for bad behavior. The call is for trust, trust in a sovereign God who always holds out hope the Created will learn the difference between good and evil. For now, let us go forth and learn!

New and fresh every morning is your love, great God of the universe; lift me when I stumble and begin to believe too much in myself. Forgive me for the countless ways I have failed to live as you have called me. Fill my heart with understanding for others and acceptance of your sovereignty in all things, even those I do not understand. And above all other concerns in my life; make your will the greatest desire of my heart. Through Jesus Christ, who lives and reigns over all, AMEN.

***

Day 28

I thank Christ Jesus our Lord, who has given me strength to do his work. He considered me trustworthy and appointed me to serve him, even though I used to blaspheme the name of Christ. In my insolence, I persecuted his people. But God had mercy on me because I did it in ignorance and unbelief. Oh, how generous and gracious our Lord was! He filled me with faith and love that come from Christ Jesus. 1 Tim 1:12-14 (NLT)

"Let us remain as empty as possible so that God can fill us up." Mother Teresa

When we boil it all down, when we burn away the chaff, when we clean out the obstructions, and when we smelt away the scrap: What do we have? We have the purified and refined nature that God created. Be it a precious metal, or a gem, the impurities of the world take away from the beauty. Our lives are this way as well. So often we clutter our minds with worthless thoughts and concerns. This only serves to dominate our lives and make less room for God. The result is each day begins, not with time spent in prayer and meditation on the Word, it begins with fretting over how this or that will get accomplished. Or, how this bill will get paid, how a relationship will go, or who's going to fix that! Worry, fret and concern dominate and God gets pushed out of our lives.

The Christian life is just like any other, except for the number one priority. The Christian life is about keeping the main thing the main thing! You see, the One who has given us everything we have, even the ability to live, is the One who deserves our time and attention. And here's the benefit; making time for the One, God, makes less room for the concerns that weigh our spirit down. They don't disappear, but they become manageable. Wouldn't everyone prefer to worry less, and feel happy about life? Absolutely! And the formula for success, in feeling happy in life is simple: first, before anything else, add God!

Lord God, become my Sabbath today. Help me empty my mind and heart of the needless worries of this life. You provide all I need, I want for nothing: so why do I fret and worry? When my concerns are banished from my heart there is space for you. Come Holy Spirit come, fill me with peace, love, joy, patience and self-control. Make me one with you as I begin another day. Walk with me and I shall be content, filled me with Sabbath thoughts and rest. Through Christ, who strengthens me I pray. AMEN

***

Day 29

Humans can reproduce only human life, but the Holy Spirit gives birth to spiritual life. So don't be surprised when I say, 'You must be born again.' The wind blows wherever it wants. Just as you can hear the wind but can't tell where it comes from or where it is going, so you can't explain how people are born of the Spirit. Jn 3:6-8 (NLT)

"I have no idea where I am going. I do not see the road ahead of me. I cannot know for certain where it will end." Thomas Merton

It was an hour after sundown and nine weary travelers, after riding their motorcycles more than 900 miles, arrived at the remote mountain road that leads to the house they had rented in the Ozarks, called Creeks End. What lay ahead was six miles of rough gravel, the occasional rock jutting out, switch backs and steep hills to climb. Forward they pressed, at one point the group was spread out so far that the last three bikes lost sight of the rest of the group. Suddenly they crested the next hill only to see the road split in three directions. What to do? They stopped, thought about waiting for someone to come back, pondered whether or not to press ahead and gamble, or give up and turn around. Then, up on a tree half covered by leaves, there it was, a sign, "Creeks End" with an arrow pointing the way. Onward they pressed and soon they caught the rest of the group stopped and waiting for them. "How much farther do we have to go?" They asked.

"We have three miles more." The answer came. Feelings of dread came over everyone. None the less, they pressed onward. After another thirty minutes, there in the distance, lights: Can it be, are we there? But as they rounded the last curve there it was, the final obstacle. Due to the heavy rains the creek was overflowing its banks and, literally, six inches of water was flowing over the top of the concrete slab used to cross. Another decision had to be made. Turn around and endure six miles of rough road for an additional 45 to 60 minutes, or plow through the water on motorcycles, each worth between $6,000 and $15,000?

Suddenly the lead bike drove in, one by one the others followed. Three bikes stalled just short of the opposite side, everyone was soaked. The steep climb on the other side was not more than one hundred feet long. They finally made it. After entering the house everyone agreed. Call the owner, ask for our money back, and stay in a hotel somewhere.

The next morning, in the daylight, everyone discovered the beautiful Ozark setting around them. All they could say is, "WOW!" The morning mountain air was amazing, the water had receded and the slab now had very little water running over it. The house, almost four star quality. All of this was not visible in the darkness. Now, rather than thinking about getting out of the deal, the decision they had to make was, how to work it out and stay.

We never know the full story until we have enough light to see what is truly before us. Jesus said; "I am the light…" Jesus opens eyes and gives us enough light to realize everything around us. Knowing the peace that all is well and most likely better than we can see, it is a spiritual health issue, not an issue for the moment. What do you see today?

Father in heaven; in this world where maps and signs from human hands are what guide us, give me confidence in your direction. I release my unhealthy need to know where I am going and why. Give me work to do for you and fulfillment in your call. I trust you to decide what comes next because you have forgiven me and prepared me for everything before me. Shield and protect me today as I seek to follow you and bless those who cross my path in the full mercy and love of your presence. Through Christ I pray. AMEN

Day 30

By his divine power, God has given us everything we need for living a godly life. We have received all of this by means of his marvelous glory and excellence. And because of his glory and excellence, he has given us great and precious promises. These are the promises that enable you to share his divine nature and escape the world's corruption caused by human desires.
2 Pt 1:3-4 (NLT)

"If Christ be risen, ye ought then to die unto the world, and to live wholly unto God." John Wesley

Life's journey takes us many places, for some the experience is spectacular and others it's simple. However, for all people the journey has a clear beginning and an end. This life is temporary but life in Christ is eternal. Does that mean we should not live out our earthly lives with gusto? Absolutely not, God calls us to put every ounce of effort into living the life we have been given to its fullest.

Joe was one of those who lived life to its fullest. He rode motorcycles; he rode horses, hunted, fished and played many sports. In his lifetime he parachuted out of airplanes, hang glided, he hiked through the mountains with nothing but a backpack and a tent. Joe was definitely a man who knew how to live life. But then, when he was in the prime years of his life, Joe's wife noticed a slight twitch in his cheek. Gradually the twitch became greater, and then his hands began shaking slightly. Joe realized he needed to see a doctor. After a series of tests the diagnosis was in, Joe had Parkinson's disease. The symptoms progressed rapidly and within three years Joe was forced to move to a medical care facility. The life of adventure and thrill had now become a life of struggle, in need of help for every day. Another nine years passed and then Joe's life, a life that had truly been lived to its fullest, came to an end.

For Joe, however, this was not a tragic or even depressing end. For Joe, his life had really begun the day he accepted Christ. You see, Christ within him had allowed him to live life to its fullest, for the right reason. Joe didn't live for himself, he lived for Christ and he made certain everyone knew it. People watched Joe put just as much effort into developing his spiritual life as he did his physical life. The spiritual, however, provided far more security and peace than the physical and when the physical began to fail the spiritual strength he had developed allowed him to continue living life to its fullest. Jesus said; "I will give you life, abundant life." So live life to its fullest!

Create in me a pure heart, O LORD, and renew a right spirit within me. Set my feet upon a path that leads, always, to your heart that I may worship you with every breath I take. I thank you for the many ways you have blessed my life, with family and friends for fellowship along the journey. I ask for my eyes to see only the things you bring me, and my desire to be solely for your will and goals. All of this I pray in the name of the One who has saved me and sustains me. Christ our Lord. AMEN!

***

Day 31

Then the LORD said to Moses, "Look, I'm going to rain down food from heaven for you. Each day the people can go out and pick up as much food as they need for that day. I will test them in this to see whether or not they will follow my instructions. On the sixth day they will gather food, and they will prepare it, there will be twice as much as usual." Ex 16:4-5 (NLT)

"I make myself rich by making my wants few." Thoreau

Details are what God does best. Think about it, when we plan for a gathering of friends or family we try to think of every detail. We plan menus, we plan accommodations, we also plan activities. But there always seems to be one thing or one aspect of our gathering that we forget to plan for. And, O yes, there are also the difficult people we have to deal with the "EGR's". What is an EGR? That is a person for whom Extra Grace is Required, EGR.

Some people become an EGR because they are naturally grouchy. Some people are naturally obnoxious, some are loud, and others are persistent complainers. There are also people who, simply because they like to talk, are considered EGR's. You know the guy who actually talks to you in the elevator. You think, "Who is this guy and what could he possibly want!"

Well, maybe these EGR's are the very people God wants to bring to us, strengthening us for living life. The very person who repulses us may just be the person who changes us. Sometimes we think these times are bad times, challenging times, but I believe the benefit is in perseverance. You see, when we endure through the entire experience, we come out the other side stronger, prepared for the next time. And let's not forget the needs of the EGR, maybe they simply need someone to listen to them. We need to consider what we are doing to bless others and maybe reaching out to help will become a life changing event in that person's life. But here is the primary point; God never leaves a detail out, never forgets to provide, God always has a complete plan. We simply must be willing to obediently follow through with every opportunity, every challenge, and God will provide. And let's never forget; to God we are all EGR's!

Precious Lord, I thank you for all who journey with me, through this spiritual life. For those close; family and ancestors, friends and associates, and of course those who have been my spiritual support and guides. Lord, I thank you for teaching me how to live and love, through the example of my parents and grandparents. I thank you for teaching me why to love, by challenging me with the unlovable. And most important, I thank you for teaching me when to love by your example of loving me always. All this you provide for me from a hand of love and I give you thanks. AMEN.

***

Day 32

Stop collecting treasures for your own benefit on earth, where moth and rust eat them and where thieves break in and steal them. Instead, collect treasures for yourselves in heaven, where moth and rust don't eat them and where thieves don't break in and steal them. Where your treasure is, there your heart will be also. Matt 6:19-21 (CEB)

"...if we can give away what we love most—then we must be very wealthy indeed." Wayne Muller

In the song, "Lord of the Dance", the words say; Dance then, wherever you may be / I am the Lord of the Dance, said He! / And I'll lead you all, wherever you may be / And I'll lead you all in the Dance, said He! A dance is something that is, in reality, an identifying action. In some cultures it is actually a form of identification.

Dancing is an important aspect of African life. In the various tribes, dance is used not only as a form of recreation and entertainment, but more important, it teaches social patterns and values to the members of the community. Traditions and rules of each society are passed down from generation to generation through dance, music and storytelling. In fact, one tribe actually uses an individual's dance in place of a name for identification. When you meet them, for the first time, you are asked; "What is your dance?" and you dance for them. Your dance becomes your identification.

In our culture we can learn from this. Everybody has a dance, the decision we have to make orbits around the impression we seek to make on others. Think for a moment, when people speak of you to others they speak of what you do as a way of telling who you are. You may be a teacher and when your friend tells someone of you they refer to you as an excellent teacher, or maybe a bad teacher, either way, your actions contribute to your identity. But here is the most important dance of all; what our dance tells others about our faith in God!

Our dance for God tells the story of our faith journey. Joy and sorrow may be expressed visually and outwardly to help others understand who we are. Caring and concern may also be expressed by what we do. You've heard the expression; "Actions speak louder than words" many times, and it is true. So the question is: What do you dance for Christ?

Dear Lord, lead the way as I begin this new day. Let me follow you to the places you need me, and do what I am called to do, go where I am sent and live for you rather than myself. Bless me today with friendship, kindness, peace and rest that my life will be a blessing to all I come to know and love. Bless those who struggle today, the sick and injured, as well as the able bodied but spiritually stricken. Forgive my sins, and the sins of all your children as we seek to live a fruitful and happy life. In the name of Christ our Lord we pray. AMEN!

***

Day 33

All glory to God, who is able to keep you from falling away and bring you with great joy into his glorious presence without a single fault. All glory to him who alone is God, our Savior through Jesus Christ our Lord. All glory, majesty, power and authority are his before all time, and in the present, and beyond all time! Amen. Jude 1:24-25 (NLT)

"My need of God is absolutely clear." Hafiz

It's been said that all things are relative and, to the objective mind, it isn't too difficult to agree with that. However, to many, being objective is a real challenge. Being objective calls for an open mind open to the possibility that the world doesn't revolve around me. There's the rub because everything we experience does, in fact, have a specific impact on our life. Therefore, we are naturally inclined to being subjective, not objective.

Being subjective leads one down a road of difficulty and disappointment. A subjective life view sees all things as a potential negative impact, rather than a positive. Many times there may be high hopes for something good (positive) to happen, but ultimately, one negative hits and the entire experience becomes negative. Does this sound like the way life should be?

But let's consider an objective life. An objective life understands the reality that all things are not going to be negative, and actually sees the negative as part of the positive. Sound strange? Well consider this; when Mt. Saint Helen was blown to pieces as it erupted, thousands of acres of trees were literally laid on their sides. That was a negative for certain, however, for

Weyerhaeuser Corporation and their employees and stockholders it was a windfall profit. The logging company came in and easily cleared out the trees and processed them into the material used to build thousands of homes, furniture, and other products. Then they planted millions of seedlings to replace the fallen trees. An objective view of the massive explosion would see the benefit of the whole, a subjective view sees only the negative impact of the explosion and those trees would have simply rotted on the ground.

Is an objective view of the world easy? Absolutely not, that is why we need our faith in God. God helps us stop and take stock of every situation. God helps us see with positive eyes so our spirits are lifted, not crushed. God created us to love us and simply desires our happiness but things like earthquakes, tornados, volcanos erupting, tsunamis, and blizzards will always be happening. Bad people will always do bad things and bring pain and suffering but all of this provides yet another opportunity to trust God.

Holy God, for children I wish self-knowledge, courage, safety and joy. For loved ones and friends I wish wisdom, peace and love. I pray for all to be at peace, free from suffering, filled with happiness and joy along with the feeling of great love that can come only from you. In Christ I pray. AMEN!

***

Day 34

The king's heart is like a stream of water directed by the LORD; he guides it wherever he pleases. People may be right in their own eyes, but the LORD examines their hearts. The LORD is more pleased when we do what is right and just than when we offer him sacrifices. Prov. 21:1-3 (NLT)

When Jesus shared what we call the Sermon on the Mount, he started by taking his close disciples away for some personal teaching. That is when he shared the Beatitudes. Ironically we have always assumed he taught these principles to the large crowd that was following him. But no, he personally taught his close disciples so they would be able to teach the masses. Think about that for a moment; disciple means learner and Christ has called every believer to be a learner. What, then, do we do with what we have learned? We must teach others!

Following the Sermon on the Mount Jesus sent his disciple forth to teach and heal all who they came in contact with. Today as believers continue to learn more about Christ, their Savior, we must all remember we are not only called, we are sent.

Almighty Creator God, comfort those who mourn today and give strength to all who struggle. Make my heart full with your love and forgiveness and turn my eyes from self to others. I ask you to be my personal guide through this day so my direction is right and my decisions are sure. Bless those whose journey is difficult today and give light to show the way. AMEN

***

Day 35

Trust the LORD and do good; live in the land and farm faithfulness. Enjoy the LORD, and he will give what your heart asks. Commit your way to the LORD! Trust him! He will act and will make your righteousness shine like the dawn, your justice like high noon. Be still before the LORD, and wait for him. Ps 37:3-7 (CEB)

(From and old Hasidic poem) All of your words each day are related to one another. All of them rooted in the first words you speak.

Trust, something we do regularly, sometimes unconsciously. For example; when we cross a bridge, either on foot or in our cars, we trust the bridge will not collapse. In America we have a sort of entitlement attitude, as if we are entitled to a safe bridge. That is why we are so shocked when a bridge collapses. We also trust there will be air to breath, we almost never consider what we would do if we become short of oxygen. We trust our friends and family each day and may go very long times without questioning them. However, when trust is broken it requires much more time to rebuild.

We can trust God, even when we experience tragic losses. The story of Job, in the Old Testament is sometimes presented as a message of patience, and it is. Job patiently endured trial after trial and almost made it without questioning God. But the story of Job can best described in one word, trust. You see, God expected Job to trust that all would be well, and it was. The question for us today is: How well do we trust the God who loves us?

God of the day and night; give me peace today, so I may live in your joy. Give me strength today, so I may feel the confidence of walking with you. Give me grace today and remind me of your forgiveness. And give me courage today, that I may share your love with all I see. This I pray in the name of the Risen Christ. AMEN!

***

Day 36

Jesus replied, "The most important one [commandment] is Israel, listen! Our God is the one Lord, and you must love the Lord your God with all your heart, with all your being, with all your mind, and with all your strength. The second is this, You will love your neighbor as yourself. No other commandment is greater than these. Mk 12:29-31 (CEB)

"To seek help we turn to the One who created us, formed us, and loves us where we are and yet always seeks to lead us to become more than we are." Bishop Rueben P. Job

The year was 1666, a young Frenchman named Nicholas Herman, had been serving as a footman and a soldier, began yearning for more meaning to his life. He was uneducated and had no skills whatsoever, but in his heart he knew he needed to do something with his life. He did the only thing he knew, he prayed. What happened to him was something totally unexpected, God completely changed his heart. Now, rather than yearning for meaning in his life he desired one thing only, to be close with God.   He joined an order of Monks, the barefooted Carmelites, as a lay brother and he was assigned to work in the kitchen and his name given, Brother Lawrence.

Brother Lawrence was thrilled with the opportunity to work in the kitchen. He never preached, he never led people to Christ personally. However, his letters written to a friend, later published in 1897 no doubt has helped many find their way to a closer walk with Christ. Brother Lawrence had one simple desire, to be close with God, even when he was washing dishes. He once said; "If I dare use this expression, I should choose to call this state the bosom of God, for the inexpressible sweetness which I taste and experience there."

The message of Brother Lawrence is a simple one, for certain. Life is not about accomplishments and success, life is about drawing near to God. Close communion with the One who created me, a simple walk, hand in hand, with the Master, the Gentle Healer from Nazareth, my Savior and my King.

Come Holy Spirit come into my life today so I may know you with absolute intimacy. Help me feel you in the silence, in the air I breathe, and on the ground I walk. Speak your comforting words of forgiveness and assurance to me once more, that I may love you, my Lord and God. Carry me through this day as I commit my way to you, a way of love and understanding for self and others. In the name of the gentle Healer from Nazareth I pray. AMEN!

***

Day 37

As God's chosen ones, holy and beloved, clothe yourselves with compassion, kindness, humility, meekness, and patience. Bear with one another and, if anyone has a complaint against another, forgive each other; just as the Lord has forgiven you, so you also must forgive. Above all, clothe yourselves with love, which binds everything together in perfect harmony. Col 3:12-14

"Whatever is foreseen in joy must be lived out from day to day." Wendell Berry

We are all called to ministry, not just the professional clergy but every Christian. In fact, the real job of the clergy, or pastor, is not to do all the ministry of the church, the real job of the pastor is to equip the members of the church to do ministry. When Jesus said, "Don't be afraid. From now on, you will be fishing for people." (Lk 5:10) He was setting the stage for teaching his disciples how to be in ministry.

Disciple means "learner" and Rabbi, "teacher"; so Jesus, the teacher, was teaching the disciples, the learners. If there were no ending result or action associated with the learning, the learning would be pointless. So, Jesus was teaching the Disciples how to do the work of ministry, after all, He was only with them for three years. Today, twenty centuries later, every Christian is a disciple, learning from Jesus Christ, through pastors, how to do the ministry He has called us to do. Our pastors are our leaders, equipping all Christians to do the work of ministry in the world.

Where is God calling you to ministry today? Who do you see struggling and in need? What situation have you observed and thought; 'someone should do something to help'. Well, consider this, for every need in which we think 'someone' should do something, and we fail to act, the 'someone' becomes 'no one' and that is simply tragic. God calls us to be the 'someone' and God's heart is broken when we settle for being the 'no one'!

Heavenly Father; Today I look to you for the certainty of hope in Jesus Christ: Hope that fuels my desire to be one with all Believers: Hope that fuels my desire to see you at work, in my life and others. Enable my way of living to be life giving, not life draining. And guide me to a way of enhanced living for you and those I meet along the journey, for your forgiveness has provided the greatest possible life for me today. In the name of your blessed Son, Jesus Christ, I pray. AMEN!

***

Day 38

For the whole law can be summed up in this one command: "love your neighbor as yourself." But if you are always biting and devouring one another, watch out! Beware of destroying one another. So I say, let the Holy Spirit guide your lives. Then you won't be doing what your sinful nature craves. Gal 5:14-16 (NLT)

"We cannot trust ourselves too much, because we often lack grace and understanding." William C. Creasy

There is a simple formula for the complete Christian life; love God and love the people God loves! Think about it, even the birds, animals, and the fish of the sea were created to be loved. In Genesis God said; "take dominion…" not meaning forceful possession but thoughtful stewardship of all living creatures. Thoughtful stewardship is another phrase for love! How could anyone deny the love of God when taking inventory of the things God has created and the good each provides for humankind? Through all these things God provides; food, medicine, clothing, shelter, preservatives, tools, transportation, entertainment, comfort, and even companionship. This is not even an exhaustive list; we could go on and on.

Now for the difficult part, cute and cuddly animals are easy to love but some people, well we all know, are very difficult to love. But wait, God says 'love your neighbor' so maybe that troublesome kid across town is not mine to love, or that terrorist, or that child molester, thief, drug addict etc. Sorry, we can't get off that easy. In Luke's version of Jesus' story of the Good Samaritan (Lk 10:25-37), Jesus tells the story in response to a man asking what he needs to do to inherit eternal life.. Jesus says 'love God, love your neighbor'! To which the man asks: 'Who's my neighbor?' Jesus then shares the story of the Good Samaritan, despised and hated as well as shunned from society, who turned out to be the one who helped, loved, his neighbor. The answer Jesus gave is this; every person God has created is MY neighbor. And God loves every one of them, yes even the evil ones, even the dirty, the disgusting, the mean, nasty, addicted, criminals, you name them and God loves them. God is waiting for the opportunity to show His love for them, and God can only show His love for them through you and me! A pre-believer cannot see, or know, God's love but they can see, know and feel love from us and our call is to show them that it's God's love we share.

Loving God, I thank you for proving your love for me through your gift of the life death and resurrection of your Son Jesus Christ. Now I ask you to help me live as He lived, fully trusting in your goodness and love. Help me set aside the habits I have formed which separate me from you. Replace my selfish ways with the ways of Christ so I will be a blessing to all who are near me, and not a burden. Continue to work your grace in my life and help me practice what You have exemplified in all You do in the name of the One and only Christ. AMEN!

***

Day 39

Unless it is the LORD who builds the house, the builders work is pointless. Unless it is the LORD who protects the city, the guard on duty is pointless. Ps 127:1 (CEB)

"His servant I am, and, as such, am employed according to the plain direction of his word." John Wesley

How many of us remember the somewhat silly saying, "Stop the world, I want to get off!"? Well silly as it may be, sometimes it is a desire brought on by the circumstances we see around us. This world is filled with difficulty, many lack adequate food, shelter and clothing, the very things the affluent take for granted. But giving up solves nothing and, in reality, does nothing more than hand the victory over to the forces of evil. There must be a better way of living in a world so beaten down, so nearly defeated.

In the 18th century, John Wesley saw a world in trouble, times change but seldom, Wesley's world was just like our today. Everyone was yearning for a better, more fulfilled life. Even those caught up in the evil of the day knew there had to be a better life, even for them. Wesley presented a new way of looking at life, life based on three simple rules, as he called them. Are you ready to learn how simple a good life is? Here you go, Three Simple Rules: DO NO HARM—DO GOOD—STAY IN LOVE WITH GOD.

Now you have it, the simple formula for a better life, not a perfect life, but a life much more fulfilling than the way of the world. Think about these simple rules today, ponder the implications for your life, and everyone around you, as you practice them. Then, tomorrow, consider what each means for you, one at a time.

Dear God, I ask you for a blessing today, for family and those whose love has changed my life, and for all your creation. I pray for comfort for those who struggle, for peace in the lives of those who are tormented, and for joy in the lives of all whose lives are bound by sorrow. I pray for healing for the sick and injured, as well as, all who struggle with addiction. And, O God, may we all feel the warmth of your love and forgiveness in our hearts. In Christ I pray. AMEN!

***

Day 40

When they finished eating, Jesus asked Simon Peter, "Simon son of John, do you love me more than these?" Simon replied, "Yes, Lord, you know I love you." Jesus said to him, "Feed my lambs." Jn 21:15 (CEB)

"It seems easier to be God than to love God, easier to control people than to love people, easier to own life than to love life." Henry Nouwen

How often do we stop and take a careful look at ourselves and how we interact with others? For some this may never occur, but the Christian life is more than what impacts "me", the Christian life is focused outward, making it about others rather than self. Outward focus is what Christ demonstrated for us and from this we observe patience, kindness and self-control, three virtues we rarely cultivate in our lives.

The first of Wesley's Three Simple Rules can help us keep our interactions with others peaceful and fruitful. DO NO HARM is a way of life, not merely a motto or even a goal. Think about it, if I consciously seek to do no harm I will carefully weigh every word before speaking. I will always consider the consequences for what I am about to do, and I will fashion my life based on pro-action rather than re-action. To do no harm means I will be on guard so my actions, words, and even silence will do nothing to add injury to one of God's children.

Some may say; 'that's not normal', but to the Christian this is normal as it is in keeping with the life Jesus Christ has called us to. Doing no harm becomes the positive cost, otherwise known as profit, of discipleship. Jesus said, "For which of you, intending to build a tower, does not first sit down and estimate the cost, to see whether you have enough to complete it?" (Lk 14:28) Think about it, what would your relationships be like today if everything you do is preceded by the thought of not doing harm in any way? I dare say things will improve, for you and those you know and love. There is a cost to every decision we make for Christ, but the greatest cost is positive cost and when we commit to do no harm Christ wins, our neighbor wins, the people we love win, the people we meet for the first time win, and we win!

Teach me your way of love, O God, so my walk with you will be a walk of joy and harmony, not trial and struggle. Give me a heart of understanding and compassion where the world calls for judgment and scorn. Give me a mind and spirit of forgiveness, just as you have forgiven me, and may your name be shouted from the mountain tops by the actions of my life each and every day. Through Christ who strengthens me. AMEN!

***

Day 41

Brothers and sisters, we urge you to warn those who are lazy. Encourage those who are timid. Take tender care of those who are weak. Be patient with everyone. See that no one pays back evil for evil, but always try to do good to each other and to all people. Always be joyful. Never stop praying. Be thankful in all circumstances, for this is God's will for you who belong to Christ Jesus. 1 Thess. 5:14-18 (NLT)

"Fix some part of every day for private exercises...Whether you like it or no, read and pray daily. It is for your life; there is no other way..." John Wesley

Why wait? Why wait for the need to be expressed, or the tragedy to occur? Why wait, for the obvious to be expressed? As Nike's marketing campaign for athletic shoes says; 'Just Do It!' I am referring to the need to DO GOOD, the second of John Wesley's 18th century rules for Christian living. Doing good, like doing no harm, is a proactive way of living. That's what Jesus was referring to when he said, "But I say to you that listen, Love your enemies, do good to those who hate you, bless those who curse you, pray for those who abuse you." (Lk 6:27-28) So, as you can see, doing good is both a serious challenge, and a command from Jesus Christ. Yikes! How are we to accomplish this one?

Doing good is a way of life, and this way of living requires that we take a careful assessment of how we are living, every day. It starts with a firm commitment; from now on I am dedicating my life to make life better for everyone around me! Now the assessment, I may start with family and ask: How am I doing? Then I need to evaluate my assessment, hopefully I will find that I am doing good toward and for them. Then, expand the assessment outward to friends, co-workers, and ultimately the stranger I meet and even those who hate me. Yes, this includes everyone, not just the easy people to do good things for, even that guy who cut you off in traffic! Yes, even the rotten to the core are loved by God.

Bishop Rubin Job once said; "Every act and every word must pass through the love and will of God and there be measured to discover if its purpose does indeed bring good and goodness to all it touches." God says, in the Bible, that the rains fall on the fields of the evil just as the fields of the righteous showing us that God loves all people. So, why would we, as Christians, not desire to do good for all of the people God loves? Does that mean they will always say thank you? No, in fact many will never acknowledge your good deeds, but our desire to do good must never be motivated on the response you will receive from people. Our motivation is the love of God, that's all. Now, 'Just Do It!'

Great and loving Teacher; make your home in my heart today, and stay within me all day long guarding and guiding me from my foolish ways and decisions. Help me today, to be an answer to another person's prayer and thus be a sign of your grace, love and forgiveness. Make me a sign of hope for the world you have created and sustained. In your precious name I pray. AMEN!

***

Day 42

I'm fully satisfied as with a rich dinner. My mouth speaks praise with joy on my lips – whenever I ponder you on my bed, whenever I meditate on you in the middle of the night because you've been a help to me and I shout for joy in the protection of your wings. Ps 63:5-7 (NLT)

"Thou art the strength of my heart and my portion forever." John Wesley

The third of John Wesley's Three Simple Rules is; STAY IN LOVE WITH GOD. Many will say this means living a life cultivated by the Spiritual Disciplines. And, according to Wesley, they are correct. John Wesley believed in rising early and spending time with God. He considered himself in need of constant prayer so his day was filled with multiple times of prayer. Perhaps the greatest benefit of Spiritual Disciplines is the many ways we acknowledge the importance of living life for something bigger than ourselves.

In a book titled "The Illuminated Life" Joan Chittister writes; "All we have in life is life. Things – the cars, the houses, the jobs, the money – come and go, turn to dust between our fingers, change and disappear....the secret of life...is that it must be developed from the inside out." Living life from the inside out is only possible with a close, intimate, relationship with God. This requires scripture meditation, prayer, fellowship, worship, and service. Staying in love with God is simply this; staying close to God!

So today, reach out to God. Take the hand of God, who loves you. Jump into the arms of love and allow your Heavenly Father to nurture as He holds you. Stay in love with God by worshiping Him, sing to Him, call out to Him and seek Him. Stay in love with God and you will find your life naturally becoming a life lived by Wesley's Three Simple Rules; DO NO HARM, DO GOOD, and STAY IN LOVE WITH GOD!

Loving Savior; I ask you today for the direction and guidance to live as you live, to love as you love and to serve as you serve. Empower my heart with your words of assurance and kindle the fire of Your Spirit within me. Send your blessing upon all who love you this day, and may your will be done, here and now. Through the name and presence of Jesus Christ, AMEN!

***

Day 43

Create in me a clean heart, O God. Renew a loyal spirit within me. Do not banish me from your presence, and don't take your Holy Spirit from me. Restore to me the joy of your salvation, and make me willing to obey you. Ps 51:10-12 (NLT)

It's been said that we have a sinful nature, that we can't possibly be good. Well, as humans we are sinful but it is not our nature to sin, we have learned to sin. When God created humanity, man and woman, we were created without sin; in fact we did not even know how to sin! So our nature is to live without sinning, which would make for a pretty easy life if not for one radical course adjustment that happened shortly after creation.

Evil, coupled with our gift of free-will, a gift God gives out of love, combined to result in our nature falling. So while it is incorrect to say sin is our nature, it is correct to say our nature is fallen! Evil, or Satan, which means "Evil One", is in the world and has been since God created all things. Why is evil in the world? Because God, who created all things, also created evil, Satan is a creation of God! Therefore Satan is inferior to God, as just one of God's creations. But wait: How could God do such a thing? The reality is, we would have no way of recognizing what is good if there was nothing evil, so evil is necessary to provide contrast in this world. Is it God's will that people do evil things? No, it is always God's desire that His people will be good, and flee evil. But, since we live in an evil environment, we are susceptible to evil's influence and impact, on our lives and others.

Rick Warren, of Saddleback Church, once likened our spiritual environment to the ocean. The fish swimming in the salt water of the Pacific Ocean cannot live in any other environment. The fish is surrounded by salt water. Like the fish, we swim in a sea of evil and sin so we cannot avoid its influence. Evil is all around us but that does not mean we cannot be saved from it. Jesus Christ is our protection from sin, just as Satan is pure evil Jesus Christ is pure good. We will be tempted, and because God loves us so much and blesses us with free-will, there will be times when people, not God, do bad things and cause harm to the innocent. But we can take heart, because God always has an eternal answer to the temporary things of this world, God always has the final

Word, if you will. Jesus Christ crucified and risen, and that's all we need!

Great and gentle Spirit; make your presence known to me in this special time of prayer and reflection. Make me keenly aware of my failures and confident in your eternal desire to forgive me. Heal my wounds and mend my broken spirit. I ask You, Holy Spirit, to make me whole, complete and at total peace with your will, my neighbor and myself. In Christ, my true strength, I pray. AMEN!

**

Day 44

Many people say, "We can't find goodness anywhere. The light of your face has left us, LORD!" But you have filled my heart with more joy than when their wheat and wine are everywhere! I will lie down and fall asleep in peace because you alone, LORD, let me live in safety. Ps 4:6-8 (CEB)

"Through your grace I promise that neither life nor death shall part me from you." Wesley's Covenant Prayer

A young mother once related a story, a true story, about her experience with her son when her daughter was born. It seems that her three year old son wanted to spend some time, alone, with his newborn sister. Well, the young mother was very reluctant to allow this, and she discussed it with her husband and they decided to tell their little boy it would be best if he waited until his sister was a bit older. After all, they were thinking, they remembered the pre-birth class they attended that focused on sibling rivalry and the potential for the older sibling to harm the newborn. So, because of their fear, they decided it was not a good idea. But the three year old boy persisted.

"Please, I want to talk to my sister, alone!" He cried to his mother. This went on over and over again, slowly wearing his mother down. So one day, after several days of relentless requests, when the father returned from work the parents decided they would allow the boy time alone with his newborn sister, but they would make sure the baby monitor was on and they would listen carefully for any sign of trouble.

The little boy was ecstatic. He walked into his sister's room and slowly approached the crib against the wall. He turned and looked back at his parents, nervously watching through the doorway. They quietly closed the door and rushed over to the side of the baby monitor to listen. There was silence, and then the boy spoke.

"Tell me about Jesus," he whispered to his sister, "'cause I'm starting to forget." He asked her several more times and then, when it was clear to him that she could not yet tell him he said, "OK, I'll wait until you're a little older." With that he turned and walked out of the room, his parents opened the door; he passed by them without uttering a word. He went to his toys and began to play, never asking again to talk with his sister alone.

Stories like this are proof that God has known us since before we were born, as the Psalmist writes; "You watched me as I was being formed in utter seclusion, as I was woven together in the dark of the womb." (Ps 139:15 NLT) Can this story be confirmation of these words? Yes, God has known you since before you were born, you probably don't remember it, like the little boy did, but you were held in the arms of Jesus then carefully, and lovingly, placed in your parents arms. And even if your childhood was filled with difficulty know this; God has never stopped loving you and longing to hold you again!

Jesus, you were with me when I struggled and you were with me when I succeeded. Comfort, peace and grace accompany your forgiveness and my life is new every day in you. I confess I am not faithful to your call, at every opportunity. Make fresh your message of love in my life today and make my life an instrument of your hand, today and every day. AMEN!

***

Day 45

Our lives are in Christ like fragrance rising up to God. But this fragrance is perceived differently by those who are being saved and by those who are perishing. To those who are perishing, we are a dreadful smell of death and doom. But to those who are being saved, we are a life giving perfume. And who is adequate for such a task as this? 2 Cor. 2:15-16 (NLT)

Serving God is about responding to God's love. God's love is a flowing love, the spring of life welling up within our hearts. When you think of that image, a spring is a source a source which begins a journey. In Israel the Sea of Galilee, sometimes referred to as Lake Gennesaret, is completely spring fed. Oh there is run off from the mountains when there is rain, but the springs provide the bulk of the water. Out of the lake flows the Jordan River, southward. As the river winds its way south it provides life giving water to the Kibbutz, the small self-contained farm communities and on through Jericho. Eventually the river empties into the Dead Sea, 2000 feet below sea level.

In the Dead Sea, literally nothing lives, no fish, no plant life, not even bacteria. The water has a pungent smell of tar. The Romans named the Dead Sea, "Lake Asphaltus" due to this smell and the greasy feel of the water. Geologically there are many reasons for the lack of life in the Dead Sea but all are a result of fact that the waters, the life giving waters, of the Jordan River are forever halted when entering the sea. You see, the Dead Sea has no outlet; water flows in but does not flow out. The water is stagnant, left to absorb the minerals, 2000 feet below sea level and literally die.

In our lives, God's love flow in for the ultimate purpose of flowing through us in order to provide life to the others, downstream. Unfortunately our human condition is such that we prefer to keep it to ourselves. But, where would we be if every faithful servant of Christ before us had the same attitude? For example; the Apostle Paul traveled on three missionary journeys in his life. He covered, in all, about 1200 miles on these trips, sometimes retracing his steps. Paul allowed the love of God to flow through him and into the lives of devoted Christians and then he moved on. What an example for each of us!

Maybe today, being just a bit more mindful of the awesome gift God has placed in your heart, you too will allow God's love to flow through you and into someone's life. Be a source of life, not a dead end. Be the one who offers help, and not the one who walks away. Above all, be the servant Christ needs to change this world!

Holy God, today I ask you for the courage to serve you. Please shield me from my fears, protect me from my spiritual weakness, and cover me with your blessing of confidence. I pray for those who will not believe me today, give them peace as they too struggle to understand and to know you fully. I ask you to bless those whose lives are interrupted by tragedy, clouding their ability to know your mercy and goodness. I ask you to heal the brokenhearted and strengthen those who mourn. And, as always, forgive my sins and the sins of all your children, through Jesus Christ I pray. AMEN!

***

Day 46

When the cool evening breezes were blowing, the man and his wife heard the LORD God walking about in the garden. So they hid from the LORD God among the trees. Then the LORD God called to the man, "Where are you?" Gen 3:8-9 (NLT)

God is looking, seeking, and searching for the very souls He created. There's a certain curiosity raised by this reality. From a Christian perspective one would find it ridiculous, perhaps even offensive for the child to desire no contact with the parent and yet, when we avoid God we are intentionally doing just that. Thus is the tragedy of sin! Sin separates, when we do something bad to someone we deepen the gap that separates us, and when someone does something bad to us, we do the same.

After all, we really have no reason to desire a closer relationship with a person who has brought us harm.

Here is where God differs in such a situation. God is love! You see, God knows what makes us tick, if you will, and because God knows us so well God will continue to seek us, even when we have ignored, insulted and run away. Why? Because God is love! As the apostle writes, "Love is patient and kind. Love is not jealous or boastful or proud or rude. It does not demand its own way. It is not irritable, and it keeps no record of being wronged. It does not rejoice about injustice but rejoices whenever the truth wins out. Love never gives up, never loses faith, is always hopeful, and endures through every circumstance." (1 Cor. 13:4-7)

Oh, did I mention God is love? Because God is love God will always look for you and me, even when we don't want to be found, what a thought. So take heart today because no matter how we respond to God, positive or negative, God still loves us! That is real peace of mind!

Dear Jesus, every day I want to look for you, as you look for me. Help me find my way in this strange land so I can serve you as you deserve. Send your blessing upon all who worship you today, and may my life represent you faithfully and properly, as a forgiven and empowered servant. This I pray in your Holy and Living name. AMEN!

***

Day 47

"I, Jesus, have sent my angel to give you this message for the churches. I am both the source of David and the heir to his throne. I am the bright morning star." The Spirit of the bride says, "Come." Let anyone who hears this say, "Come." Let anyone who is thirsty come. Let anyone who desires drink freely from the water of life. Rev 22:16-17 (NLT)

"Thou art my master, and Thy name is Truth, and Truth shall be my abiding name till I die." Sojourner Truth

Life can become completely cluttered with the desire to survive. How ironic it is, we are God's people and yet we seem to live with worry filled days always concerned about how we will survive or how we can manage the day. Jesus addressed this flaw in our human condition by offering peace; "What's the price of a pet canary? Some loose change, right? And God cares what happens to it even more than you do. He pays even greater attention to you, down to the last detail—even numbering the hairs on your head! So don't be intimidated by all this bully talk. You're worth more than a million canaries." (Matt 10:29-31 MSSG)

What do we have to worry about? God will provide, and cares for us; this is the promise of Christ, Messiah, Savior. But life is filled with reasons not to trust God; maybe we should view the challenges of everyday life in a different light. How about the Light of Christ? The next time life deals a hand that draws attention to the need, and the negative, look at it as an opportunity to bring a gift to Jesus. Yes, when we give our burdens to Christ it is a gift we give. Look again at

His words; "Let anyone who is thirsty come. Let anyone who desires drink freely from the water of life." (Rev. 22:17) This promise is real! God does want our problems because God can take care of us and longs to without condition, without reservation. Why? You've heard it before now listen carefully; God loves YOU!

Master, deliver me from the bondage of my earthly thoughts and aspirations. Set my sights on your will and direction so I may serve you in full and complete faith. Rain your blessing on all the earth today and make, for all, a way to come to you, using my life in the complete work of Your Kingdom. And, as always, forgive my many sins, both known and unknown to my mind. In Christ I pray. AMEN!

***

Day 48

I have given you an example to follow. Do as I have done to you. I tell you the truth, slaves are not greater than their master. Nor is the messenger more important than the one who sends the message. Now that you know these things, God will bless you for doing them. Jn 13:15-17 (NLT)

"Learn the lesson that, if you are to do the work of a prophet, what you need is not a scepter but a hoe." Bernard of Clairvaux

From time to time we all need a reality check, a time of total objectivity, without this we will consistently justify our actions, the good and the bad. For example, in recent history when nations go to war inevitably one or the other will invoke the name of God as if God is on their side. In the 1990's both George H.W. Bush and Saddam Hussein said they would win the Gulf War because it is just and right before God.

Social justice advocates have taken their passion for the down trodden and preached a gospel of reparation rather than justice. Martin Marty once said; "Justice is not for just us!" and he was right but true justice is just that, justice. Justice is treating everyone fairly with the full privilege of God's love. Justice is not a call to repair the injustice of the past that requires forgiveness; and forgiveness is simply giving up the right to pay someone back.

Our greatest example is Christ. Jesus faced much opposition and he was in many situations in which he could have exploded in anger, or to use the Christianized term for anger, righteous indignation. But, there is only one instance in the Bible where we see anything close to anger from Jesus and that was the clearing of the Temple courts of the merchants and the animals he said, "The Scriptures declare, 'My Temple will be called a house of prayer,' but you have turned it into a den of thieves!" (Matt 21:13) Clearly his anger was directed toward what the people did, not the people. There is no sign of inflicting punishment or retribution on the money changers and merchants.

How did Jesus respond to those who treated him unjustly? "He was led like a sheep to the slaughter. And as a lamb is silent before its shearers, he did not open his mouth. He was humiliated and received no justice. Who can speak of his descendants? For his life was taken from the earth." (Acts 8:32-33). Jesus was led like a sheep, for the entire time of his life, and he did not lash out or even protest. And after his crucifixion how did he respond? Here it is again, He loved everyone, even those who treated him unjustly! The "sword of righteousness" is none other than God's Word, and the Word is Christ!

Jesus; breathe your breath of love in me, and inhale my devotion and praise for you. Your love is great for me and you empower my spirit through Your Holy Spirit to serve and help all your children. Reveal the needs of your children to my eyes, and remove the scales of prejudice that blind me to their suffering and pain. LORD, with your gentle presence; make me what you wish and send me where you will, as a forgiven and renewed servant. All this I pray through your loving name. AMEN!

***

Day 49

I pray that the God of our Lord Jesus Christ, the Father of glory, will give you a spirit of wisdom and revelation that makes God known to you. I pray that the eyes of your heart will have enough light to see what is the hope of God's call, what is the richness of God's glorious inheritance among believers, and what is the overwhelming greatness of God's power that is working among us believers. This power is conferred by the energy of God's powerful strength. Eph. 1:17-19 (CEB)

"That we should establish ourselves in a sense of God's presence by continually conversing with Him." Brother Lawrence

In the New Testament the people of the early first century church were called the People of the Way. Even before the term Christian was used they were seen as different. The Way was associated with a life path, one first traveled by Christ, as example for them all. The Way was one of peace and non-violence, a Way directed in patience, kindness, humility, and grace. Little wonder they were seen as weak in the eyes of the world.

The Greco-Roman culture was one based on power and status. Citizenship was carefully classified and if you were not one of the privileged, well, too bad for you. Believe it or not, this is still an issue in today's society. But, the Way is still a valid metaphor for the Christian life. You see, the Way is not a simple path or road; the Way is a philosophy of life, a life following Christ. Jesus said; "If someone slaps you on the right cheek, offer the other cheek also. If you are sued in court and your shirt is taken from you, give your coat, too. If a soldier demands that you carry his gear for a mile, carry it for two miles. Give to those who ask, and don't turn away from those who want to borrow." (Matt 5:39-42)

When Christ makes a difference in a life there is clear evidence. The question is: What evidence is there that Christ has changed my life? Ponder that for today and look for evidence of a changed attitude. How much understanding do I show people? How much grace do I show others? Am I a child of the Way, sojourning with Jesus each and every day?

Hello Lord; The pleasure and privilege of knowing you has changed my life and my world. Today I set out on a new adventure, as I do every day. My journey will not be lonely, for you are with me. My journey will not be futile, for you lead me, and my journey will not be in vain, for you have called me. You do not decide whether I am worthy for You have forgiven me, so I thank you, O God, for the high calling in Jesus Christ and for your hedge of protection around me. May your blessing rest on family, friends and acquaintances this day! In the name of the Father, the Son, and the Holy Spirit. AMEN!

***

Day 50

He said to them, "Go into the whole world and proclaim the good news to every creature. Whoever believes and is baptized will be saved, but whoever doesn't believe will be condemned." Mk 16:15-16 (CEB)

"It is an actual fact of experience that when you deepen the Christ-consciousness you deepen the God-consciousness." E. Stanley Jones

Followers of Christ, a Christian, as believers were called for the first time in first century Antioch, were persons with a new outlook on life. Just as Christ responded to criticism and ridicule with love and forgiveness Christians are called to the same. But what if it doesn't appear to be working? What if people continue to attack and chide and treat you poorly? What if all your work in sharing the love of Christ appears to be a waste of time? One answer satisfies all these questions. Sowing the seeds of Christ's love and forgiveness is always successful! Yes, always successful!

Paul says, "I planted the seed in your hearts, and Apollos watered it, but it was God who made it grow.

94

It's not important who does the planting, or who does the watering. What's important is that God makes the seed grow. The person who plants, and the person who waters work together with the same purpose. And both will be rewarded for their own hard work for we are both God's workers. And you are God's field. You are God's building." (1 Cor. 3:6-9) What Paul is saying is this; it matters not what result we see, it matters that we are sowing the seed of the Gospel as Christ has told us to do. Do we worry and fret for the ones we love who don't seem to be listening? Absolutely, we love them and we want them to listen, but rather than give up in discouragement, our disappointment is, in fact, a call to prayer. How about praying for other Christians to come and water the seed we have sown? How about praying for God to bring the rain and the nutrients so the seeds will take root and grow?

You see, when we focus on sharing the love of Christ God is able to enter in. Christ stands at the door of every soul and knocks, (Rev 3:20) and when Christians help open the door then God's Holy Spirit enters and changes that soul forever, eternally! So, take heart, don't give up, the very next knock that person hears will be Jesus!

God; open my eyes to the wonders of your creation. Make this day a holy and consecrated day to your service as I dedicate my life to you, once again. Send me to where you will, give me the work of Your Kingdom to complete, and refresh my spirit with Your Spirit, as I live in the privilege of your forgiveness. In the name of Christ I pray. AMEN!

***

Day 51

For God loved the world so much that he gave his one and only Son, so that everyone who believes in him will not perish but have eternal life. God sent his Son into the world not to judge the world but to save the world through him. There is no judgment against anyone who believes in him. But anyone who does not believe in him has already been judged for not believing in God's one and only Son. Jn 3:16-18 (NLT)

"I would suggest first, that all of you Christians, missionaries and all, must begin to live more like Jesus Christ." Mahatma Gandhi

Have you ever wondered what God sees as valuable in human beings? After all, when you compare what is with what God intended all you see is failure, and yet God still loves. Well perhaps, once again, we need to reflect on the fallen nature. For example, if you work on a computer you will know that from time to time you are unable to open a file. When the computer cannot open a file you may receive an error message like this, "unable to open file, file corrupted." Well, God created humankind with a perfect nature which became corrupted by sin. Who's to blame? Do we blame Satan, do we blame the woman and the man in the garden? Do we blame ourselves?

There is an old story about a man walking early in the morning, so early the sun had yet to rise. So he carefully felt his way in the darkness, but as careful as he was he could not avoid falling into a well. He called for help, but no one answered. So he waited and waited and eventually the sun came up. Along came a woman, she was doing her morning chore of fetching water to cook breakfast. He called to her for help. The woman looked down at the man in the well. She said, "How foolish do you have to be to fall into a well?"

"Can you help me get out?" He said.

"Sorry," she replied, "If you are foolish enough to fall in then you can find your own way out." And away she walked leaving the man in the well.

Then after a few more hours a man approached the well to get water for his horse. The man in the well called out for help. Looking down in the well the potential rescuer said, "How'd you get in there?"

"I fell in before the sun came up, I didn't see the well." said the poor man.

"According to my church's teaching, you must have sinned in order for God to punish you like this," he said, "God is punishing you for something." And he walked away.

So the man began to pray, not knowing what, or how to pray, but he knew that only God could help him. After another hour he looked up, there was another man looking down the well at him, he said nothing. Then he left, a few minutes later he reappeared and lowered a ladder down the well, again saying nothing. The well bound man hurried up the ladder and wanted to thank his silent rescuer. However, when he climbed out of the well he looked around and saw no one. He was completely alone. All he saw was a sign, it read; "Please place ladder here in case someone falls in the well." The ladder had been there all along but only one used it to rescue him.

Jesus said, "Healthy people do not need a doctor—sick people do. I have come to call not those who think they are righteous, but those who know they are sinners." (Mk 2:17 NLT) Was the man in the well foolish? Yes, but that doesn't mean God punished him. Was the man a sinner? Yes, but again, God did not punish him by throwing him in the well. Was the ladder available to the first two people as a means to rescue the man in the well? Yes, but they failed to act in mercy and grace. Will the man in the well go out of his way to rescue anyone he sees trapped in a well from now on? Absolutely, because Christ has shown him how to be a rescuer, now, go and do likewise!

O Teacher of love; teach me today to live more like you. Come down into my heart and teach me to feel the suffering of others, to serve the "leper" and "pariah" with an all-embracing love. I pray that your sorrow-laden heart will be lightened, today and every day, by the desire of my heart to follow your blessed example. As a forgiven and renewed servant of yours I pray. AMEN!

***

Day 52

Anyone who receives you receives me, and anyone who receives me receives the Father who sent me. If you receive a prophet as one who speaks for God, you will be given the same reward as a prophet. And if you receive righteous people because of their righteousness, you will be given a reward like theirs. And if you give even a cup of cold water to one of the least of my followers, you will surely be rewarded. Matt 10:40-42 (NLT)

"Ideas are poor ghosts, until they become incarnate."
George Eliot

Today is a special day, a day filled with potential for both good and evil. Think about it, when God gives us a new twenty four hour block of time He really gives it to us. Some believe God still maintains control over us as some sort of puppeteer holding the strings of movement over us. But that is theologically incorrect. But why then do we always say God is in control? Maybe it's because the Bible makes it clear that God is never out of control! "God is our refuge and strength, always ready to help in times of trouble. So we will not fear when earthquakes come and the mountains crumble into the sea. Let the oceans roar and foam. Let the mountains tremble as the waters surge!.. Be still and know that I am God! I will be honored by every nation. I will be honored throughout the world." (Ps 46:1-3, 10 NLT)

God is always prepared, never surprised, and never out of control but when God gives something to us He really gives it to us. Like today, God has completely given us this day and will not interfere with the way we use it, good or bad. The confidence we are afforded, as believers, is that we will always have God's help in using our day for good. You see, it's as if we have a bank account and God makes a daily deposit for us. The issue is simply how we spend the assets in our account. We will receive another deposit tomorrow but if we have repeatedly used each deposit for anything other than the goodness God shows us, we will grow to despise tomorrow and soon be drawn deeper and deeper into the abyss of sin and disappointment. But if we use the gift of this new day for God's glory, living after the example of Jesus, we will always look forward to the next new day.

You see, God came to us in human flesh, incarnate, for the purpose of expressing His love for us. To show us that life is livable according to His model example. Christ came to give us hope, in a world of hopelessness, and help for our helpless souls! Will we be rewarded with an easy day because we use today for good? Not necessarily, but we will be rewarded with another new day with Christ and for the Christian that is the greatest reward of all.

Loving Jesus; as the rains wash every inch of the surface of the earth, pour out your presence in my life today. I ask for courage to face the unknown and faith to face all that you call me to. Look deep into my soul and forgive even the unknown sin in my life. And I pray, not just for myself but, for all your beloved children. May your grace and peace be the soul of our existence today! In the loving and forgiving name of Christ I pray. AMEN!

***

Day 53

If you are wise and understand God's ways, prove it by leading an honorable life, doing good works with humility that comes from wisdom. Jas 3:13 (NLT)

In the classic hymn "How Great Thou Art" a verse is sung; "That on the cross, my burden gladly bearing, he bled and died to take away my sin…" These words are words of gratitude and praise for God's blessing of freedom from the bondage of sin. Where, or what, would we be were it not for the forgiveness that Christ affords us? Think for a moment of the consequences of sin. It's been said that sin begets sin and rightfully so. Each willful sin committed is revealed in its time and, in every case, either another sin is committed to cover up the first, or another sin is committed to build on it. Let's face it, we are good at sinning!

But there will come a time, for many people, when the reality of sin becomes too much to bear because the consequences begin to take a toll. Dishonesty will eventually erode relationships. Anger eats away at one's health and well-being creating higher and higher levels of stress. Deception spends all the capitol of trust and eventually the lies are discovered. Lust and debauchery serve to be the carcinogens that eat away at the character and soon the life we thought we enjoyed becomes total depravity. This is the burden humankind has become very good at building, so well in fact that the burden becomes so large we break.

When the burden reaches the breaking point some people come to the realization that God is ready to help. This is where the Christian witness is essential, without the witness of those who have walked the same road there is little hope for relief from the weight of sin. Yes, God forgives sin, but God will not force forgiveness on us; God waits for our invitation and that can only be possible if we receive the help of others who have experienced the love of God in the midst of a sinful life. Are you ready to share your story with someone at the breaking point today? If not now—when? If not you—who? If not this—what will you do to help God save a soul?

Gracious heavenly Father, reveal your love and understanding to me today. May my life be forever guided by your light and may the forgiveness of Your Spirit always rest upon me. I pray for your continued forgiveness and restoration for my soul and may all your children feel the impact of your love through the actions of my life. In Jesus' name I pray, AMEN!

**

Day 54

And so, dear friends, while you are waiting for these things to happen, make every effort to be found living peaceful lives that are pure and blameless in his sight. 2 Pt 3:14 (NLT)

"Lord, I cannot do this unless Thou enablest me; and then I received strength more than sufficient." Brother Lawrence

There is no government, or kingdom, on the face of the earth, nor throughout human history that can come close to the nature of the Kingdom of God. God is absolutely faithful in keeping His gracious covenant promise to all creation. He "executes justice for the oppressed,…gives food for the hungry,…sets the prisoner free,…opens the eyes of the blind,…lifts up those who are bowed down,…loves the righteous,…watches over the strangers,…upholds the orphan and the widow, but the way of the wicked he brings to ruin" (Ps 146:7-9; 145:13c-20; 72:10b-14) This is the vision of the Kingdom of God the Bible gives us.

Why? Why does God do all of this? Well, this is all about love, God loves each of us as though we are His only child. Nothing is reserved for later; God's love is complete this very day! And the mission of God is simply this, to make His love known to every living soul on earth! When Jesus appeared to his disciples for the last time he issued a commission, saying to all of us 'everywhere you go today, tell people about me. Show them what I have shown you, love them like I have loved you, be patient with them as I have been patient with you, and forgive ALL things they do against you, just like I have forgiven you!. Oh, and by the way, I'm going to be with you, every moment of every day forever and ever. Don't ever forget that promise!' (My paraphrase of Matt 28:19-20)

So we have Kingdom work to do today, offering hope, help, and strength to a world filled with people wandering and wondering what to do. Now, go!

Breath of Heaven, breathe upon me today. Receive my praise and thanksgiving for all you have done for me. O God, surround me with peace and understanding as I navigate this life, and bless me with the companionship and comfort that can only come by your presence, O Holy Spirit. May my sins be forgiven and my mind enriched with your vision for this life, In Jesus' Name, AMEN!

***

Day 55

"Look! I am sending my messenger, and he will prepare the way before me. Then the Lord you are seeking will suddenly come into his Temple. The messenger of the covenant, whom you look for so eagerly, is surely coming," says the LORD of Heaven's Armies." Mal 3:1 (NLT)

"Faith alone is certainty. Everything but faith is subject to doubt. Jesus Christ alone is the certainty of faith." Dietrich Bonhoeffer, (Ethics)

Has anyone ever asked you: "What's new?" This question is a common greeting and used to open up conversation. Well, Christians have an answer to this one: "What's new? I am!" This is true because God, in saving us from our sin-led lives, provides a new outlook in life. You see, ever since the original creation, the subsequent fall from grace when sin entered our lives and the separation from God's eternal presence, humanity has been in need of restoration. When we turn away from sinful ways, and turn toward God's ways (called repentance) we become a new creation.

Christ came to provide new life, a new creation, for anyone who would accept His love. Paul wrote, "What counts is whether we have been transformed into a new creation." (Gal 6:15b NLT) But how did Paul come to know this concept of new creation? Paul experienced it firsthand. He was born Saul of Tarsus, a child of Jewish privilege and enjoyed all the benefits of Roman citizenship as well. A Pharisee of Pharisees, as he once described himself, his life had become one based solely on his service to God. But little did he know that one day he would be struck blind, dependent on others to lead him, no longer able to live independently! Now, when Saul was at his lowest point in life, fully in need, Christ came to him and made of him a new creation, and restored his physical and spiritual sight. Now his name was Paul the Apostle, a representative of the Risen Christ, a new creation!

There are only two types of people reading these words right now, those who are a new creation, or those who are seeking a new creation. This new creation is not an escape from this world; it is a way to live in this world but with a fresh understanding of what real life is. God's mission of love, which started at the fall of humanity, has always been a mission to reach every single person on earth for the purpose of making them a new creation. Christ created a new nature in the lives of his twelve disciples, they in turn helped usher in a new creation for the people they encountered ultimately right up to you and me. So: What's new with you?

Christ, my Lord and Savior; Open my eyes, my heart and my mind to your words of hope. Cleanse my spirit, and wash me with Your Holy Spirit as I seek to serve as you have served. Prepare my heart as a suitable place for you to dwell, and direct my every step, bringing me experiences that will serve to build Your Kingdom, in my life and the lives of all I meet this day. In the Holy, Honorable, and Majestic Name of Jesus Christ, I pray. AMEN!

***

Day 56

Keep the Sabbath day and treat it as holy, exactly as the LORD your God commanded: Six days you may work and do all your tasks, but the seventh day is a Sabbath to the LORD your God. Don't do any work on it – not you, your sons or daughters, your male or female servants, your oxen or donkeys or any of your animals, or the immigrant who is living among you – so that your male and female servants can rest just like you. Deut. 5:12-14 (CEB)

In the morning, when you rise, the world looks fresh and new. Your spirit is fresh and new and all you can see before you is a day filled with potential: Right? Well, for those who hold to the hope that is in Christ this is absolutely true, but even they have days when it seems very far away. Life is real and the reality of life is that from time to time, no matter how firm your faith is, you're going to experience depression and discouragement. How would God have you deal with the difficult days? Well, I believe God has suggested, through the biblical record, three clear steps to coping and overcoming problems.

First, keep everything in perspective. When Jesus was tempted by Satan to turn stones into bread and solve his hunger, he responded; "People do not live by bread alone." (Lk 4:4 NLT) He put the need for food in perspective and showed Satan that his true hunger was for God.

Second, hold the problems at a distance so they don't cloud your thinking. After his temptation, Jesus went to Nazareth, his home town. He preached in the Synagogue and after he was finished the people were enraged at his honesty and they started to riot. But Jesus calmly held the problem at a distance so it would not interfere with his ministry he had yet to complete. "…he passed right through the crowd and went on his way." (Lk 4:30 NLT)

Third, give God the first position in your life. Again, when tempted by Satan to become the ruler of all the kingdoms of the earth Jesus responded; "You must worship the LORD your God and serve him only." (Lk 4:8 NLT) When we put God first; in our week (Sabbath) in our day (Sabbath) and in our every hour and minute (Sabbath) we have the ability to face any day with an attitude of praise!

God, all things in heaven and earth are yours. You who created and continue to create have, always and everywhere, prepared the very minutes in which we exist. You provide the air I breathe, and the lungs with which I inhale and exhale. Loving God, you are complete and have created the most intricate of functions which produce life on the earth. All this calls me to obedience and faithfulness. I dedicate all that I do this day to you, O God, and may your blessing continue to touch my heart, and the hearts of all your children. In Christ I lift this prayer, AMEN!

***

Day 57

It is God's will that your honorable lives should silence ignorant people who make foolish accusations against you. For you are free, yet you are God's slaves, so don't use your freedom as an excuse to do evil. Respect everyone, and love your Christian brothers and sisters. Fear God and respect the king. 1 Pt 2: 15-17

Sharing the message of Jesus Christ has always been challenging. The Apostle Paul, who some say is the greatest evangelist who ever lived, faced opposition in people who did not believe him. Paul didn't give in to his human instinct and lash out in anger; he simply made his point and allowed people to deduce for them from what he gave them. Paul respected everyone he shared the Gospel with enough to allow them to find their way to Christ.

As a Christian one of the most obvious tasks we have is to make more Christians by sharing the love of Christ. We naturally start with the people closest to us like family, friends, neighbors, etc. Unfortunately we sometimes fall into the numbers trap and all we want to do is pile up the converts so we can show God what a wonderful job we are doing. But, this may be a shock, God isn't counting how many people you and I can convert. No, God is concerned about our personal development and formation after the example of Jesus Christ. When we focus on the numbers we will be disappointed because we can never measure up to Paul or Peter, let alone any other apostle, and certainly not Christ. This frustration will lead to a loss of self-control and we begin to separate ourselves from the very people we were trying to reach.

Once, when Paul was preaching to some non-believing Jews, he gave them his best message, but they would not believe. He finally spoke to them the words of the Prophet Isaiah; "For the hearts of these people are hardened, and their ears cannot hear, and they have closed their eyes – so their eyes cannot see, and their ears cannot hear, and their hearts cannot understand, and they cannot turn to me and let me heal them." (Acts 28:27 NLT) and with that Paul announced that he was leaving to share the Gospel with other people. He did not condemn the people for not listening; he simply made it clear that he understood they would not listen. He loved them so much he refused to disrespect them and condemn.

Respect is a hard word to live by but look at it this way, before you accepted Christ and set out on this journey of faith; God respected you so much He refused to condemn you! God allowed you to find your way in the dark to the place where there is light. Our mission is to do for others the same things God has done for us!

Holy, loving and caring God; Fill my heart with your presence today. Help me see you in every experience I have today. Send me into your mission field to serve you by serving others. Forgive my feeble attempts to justify my selfish actions and give me the heart of Your Son, Jesus Christ, in whose name I pray. AMEN!

***

Day 58

From noon until three in the afternoon the whole earth was dark. At three, Jesus cried out in a loud shout, "Eloi, Eloi, Lama sabachthani," which means, "My God, my God, why have you left me?" After hearing him, some standing there said, "Look! He's calling Elijah!"... But Jesus let out a loud cry and died. Mk 15:33-35, 37 (CEB)

"We ought, without anxiety, to expect the pardon of our sins from the blood of Jesus Christ, only endeavoring to love him with all our hearts." Brother Lawrence

For some it is very difficult to accept forgiveness, harder still to forgive. But God's love is the foundation of the relationship between Creator and Created. The creation accounts we find in Genesis all point to a step by step preparation for humankind to be provided for. The earth, the atmosphere, the sun, moon and stars; the plants, the water, the birds of the air, the fish in the lakes and oceans, and all the animals that roam the earth were created with one purpose in God's mind; to provide for humankind. And considering God has created all things, even our emotions and ability to determine our own behavior perhaps the most dangerous thing God created was our free-will!

Free-will choices have led to some very difficult and challenging events in history such as wars, crimes, mistakes, and even ridiculous doctrine of the Church that led to executions. Yes, humanity has been in the process of "becoming" what God intended and along the way some tragic mistakes have been made. But think for a moment, where we would be were it not for God's forgiveness? Each mistake would be met with harsh retribution, imagine God striking a person dead and condemning them to Hell for missing Church one Sunday! After all, one of the Ten Commandments says; "Remember the Sabbath and keep it holy." If we fail to go to Church and instead hit the golf course we should expect some consequence.

Here is where God's grace comes through. You see, we do lose something when we fail in obedience to God's laws, but our loss is not from the hand of God, our loss is from our own hand. When worship is missed so too is fellowship, corporate prayer, mutual support; we miss the opportunity of experiencing continued spiritual growth and the connection with others. Yes, we lose, so God does not need to strike us down. No, instead God forgives knowing there will be more opportunities to find our way; God gives us yet another second chance. Martin Luther once wrote, "Sin with the confidence of knowing you have already been forgiven!" Did Luther mean go out and willfully commit sins? No, what he meant was, the Christian knows better than any other person that God has forgiven and therefore we should not feel discouraged when we slip and sin but we should run faithfully to the Throne of God.

So today, you have the assurance of forgiveness and God, who loves you faithfully, has no reservations about offering you the blessing of a new day. Now, we can confidently go and forgive others because we are forgiven.

Christ, my life, my all have I said thank you lately? Thank you for your proactive work of forgiveness; you forgive all sin, even before I commit it. Thank you for

111

seeing me, not for what I am but for what I can be! Thank you for sharing your presence with me so I am never alone. Thank you for filling me with your love so I am always loved, and thank you for showing me the value of forgiving others! In Your blessed name I pray. AMEN!

***

Day 59

By his divine power, God has given us everything we need for living a godly life. We have received all this by coming to know him, the one who called us to himself by means of his marvelous glory and excellence. And because of his glory and excellence, he has given us great and precious promises. These are the promises that enable us to share his divine nature and escape the world's corruption caused by human desires. 2 Pt 1:3-4 (NLT)

In the 1970's Rock and Roll song, written by Thomas Cochrane and performed by Racal Flatts, the words say; "Life's like a road that you travel on, when there's one day here, and the next day gone. Sometimes you bend sometimes you stand, sometimes you turn your back to the wind; There's a world outside every darkened door where the blues won't haunt you anymore. LIFE IS A HIGHWAY; I WANT TO RIDE IT, ALL NIGHT LONG. IF YOU'RE GOING MY WAY I WANNA RIDE IT ALL NIGHT LONG!" These words speak to a philosophy of life as a journey, and every journey has a destination. The question is: What, or where is the destination of life?

From culture to culture the definition of life varies but in every culture humanity has sought to figure out the meaning of life. In some cultures life has little value and some really heinous practices have evolved. And in still others there has been a deep need to develop the spiritual side of human existence. For the Christian the real journey doesn't begin until Christ is part of it. You see, at some point in our lives one, or more, Christians cross our path and does something good for us and we either ask, or they volunteer the reason why they did it. This goodness was done for you in Jesus' name! Then, again, by quest or offering, the answers to the natural follow up question of just who this Jesus is are provided by means of full explanation and the process of discipleship begins.

But this is merely the beginning of the highway, and much will happen in the course of the journey. There will be joy and celebration as much as there will be pain and suffering. This is the reason why, in the marriage vows, we say "I take you; for better, for worse, for richer, for poorer, in sickness and in health, till death us do part!" You see, this life's highway has but one destination, the arms of Christ, safe and secure before the Throne of God. Where exactly is this Heaven we all long for? No one knows the actual location, but those who believe know, beyond a shadow of a doubt, that wherever God is, that is where heaven is!

So, everyone has a choice; allow the evil tragedy of this world to block your highway and force you to detour, or allow God's Holy Spirit to be your guide. Can you join the song and sing? "LIFE IS A HIGHWAY; I WANT TO RIDE IT, ALL NIGHT LONG. IF YOU'RE GOING MY WAY I WANNA RIDE IT ALL NIGHT LONG!"

Great and Almighty God, by your hand my path through this life is skillfully guided. Your power and majesty seal and protect and your grace provides a way in the wilderness for my wandering soul. Come to me today; forgive my sins and feeble attempts to direct my own life. Be the vision I require to see and know you in more intimate ways. For those who struggle today to know you, may they be given clear understanding and a sense of total peace! Through Jesus Christ I pray. AMEN!

***

Day 60

At the same time Jesus was filled with the joy of the Holy Spirit, and he said, "O Father, Lord of heaven and earth, thank you for hiding these things from those who think themselves wise and clever, and for revealing them to the childlike. Yes, Father, it pleased you to do it this way. Lk 10:21 (NLT)

"It took many generations to hammer out a new understanding of God, and it's not surprising that there were often fierce disagreements along the way." Lesslie Newbegin

In a book titled, "The Open Secret" Leslie Newbigin, who was one of the world's most brilliant Missiologists, carefully describes the mission of every Christian. Many believe mission is about going to a Developing Country to help the people. Well, that is but one facet of mission. Mission is what we have been called to do, both near and far. Jesus, when he gave his disciples the Great

Commission, said; "As you go, go to all the nations and teach them to obey all my commands as I have taught you. Baptize them in the name of the Father, and of the Son, and of the Holy Spirit." (Matt 28:19-20) So, our mission is to do just that, finish the work God began at creation. That is the secret Newbigin referred to in his book.

The secret is God began, in love, a mission to redeem every human being from the condemnation of sin and continued that work in love through the life of His Son, Jesus Christ. The Son then introduced God's Holy Spirit as our mission Guide and companion so humankind will have the opportunity to know the redeeming presence of Christ in the heart. That is the secret, it is open in that it is available to everyone, it is a secret because only those who accept Christ will know and understand it.

So there you have it, you are part of a very special corps of secret tellers! As you find opportunity to introduce Jesus to others you are sharing the secret, the open secret, and you are saving souls! Today, pray for those you know who are yet to know the secret, pray for those you have yet to meet, also to know the secret. It's a secret, but it's open!

Christ, my Lord and Savior, today I seek understanding in a new way. Help me consider all the possibilities without blindness or prejudice. Set me on a journey today that takes me to places of new experience and excitement. And, above all, fill me with Your Holy Spirit for direction and guidance. In the name of the forgiving God, AMEN!

***

Day 61

Slaves obey your earthly masters with deep respect and fear. serve them sincerely as you would serve Christ. Try to please them all the time, not just when they are watching you. As slaves of Christ, do the will of God with all your heart. Eph. 6:5-6 (NLT)

"The greater perfection a soul aspires after, the more dependent it is upon divine grace." Brother Lawrence

The Kingdom of God is founded on love, and love is the foundation for obedience and respect. When God called Moses to the mountain and spoke to him through the burning bush it wasn't a loud shout, or even a noise that caught the Bedouin shepherd's attention, it was the sight of something different. "This is amazing," Moses said to himself, "Why isn't that bush burning up? I must go see it." (Ex 3:3 NLT) Moses was amazed because he saw something out of the ordinary, something different from the status quo. Can you imagine what Moses had been thinking just before seeing the bush afire? I believe the things on Moses' mind were things like family and friends he left behind in Egypt, his Hebrew heritage and what that meant to him now that he was far from the home he had known. Moses was probably also thinking of his new family, the house of Jethro, and how his role in providing for his new wife and children was a great responsibility. Moses had to be thinking about all this and his heart may have been heavy not knowing exactly what to do next. And all of a sudden he sees the bush. And from the bush God speaks to him.

How often do we long for God to speak to us as clearly as from the burning bush? Many times we find ourselves weighed down by thoughts very similar to Moses. Home, family, responsibilities, the future, our mistakes and all the other challenges of life soon become so weighty we are absorbed into our own little world, closed off from God. And then off in the distance we see it, a slight glow amidst the darkness. Maybe it's a song we've heard before, but something is different. Maybe it's the faces of our family, but something is different. Maybe it's our job as we drive in early in the morning, but something is different. Maybe it's the desk we sit at every day, but again, something is different! We see the contrast to its surroundings and we know something is up so we move closer. Now it's more obvious, for Moses it was a bush, and it was burning, but there was still something different, something that set it apart from any ordinary bush. It was burning but it was as if it was the flame and not just fuel for the flame.

Here is the point, God can speak to us through the ordinary things of this world, but in an extraordinary way. The words of a song, the faces of our family, our job, a desk, a computer, no matter what, God can speak to us through ordinary things in extraordinary ways! And the message God brings us is founded in love and built up in love. So no matter what the day's challenge may be, take heart, the God who loves you is speaking to you. Look, there in the distance, something different! You better go closer and see!

O God, who brings us from nothing to birth and life, and saves us from eternal death, Fill us with your love and grace today. Lord, touch the hearts of those who know you, as well as, those who do not know you. And may your will be done today and every day. AMEN!

***

Day 62

So they cried out to the LORD in their distress, and God brought them out safe from their desperate circumstances. God quieted the storm to a whisper; the sea's waves were hushed. Ps 107:28-29

The heritage we share with our Judeo roots has so often been overlooked in the Church today. Lammen Sanneh, in his book "Translating The Message" writes about perspective on the dual nature of our faith. He wrote, "How Jew and Gentile stood together and separately under the radical affirmation of God's action in Jesus..." and what a message this is to all of us as Christians. Standing together, One God, and standing separately, First Covenant/Second Covenant, or Testament if preferred. There is a clear difference in our faith perspectives and yet also a profound similarity which God has built upon. With this Sanneh describes the advantage Christianity has had over Judaism, the image of "Christian mission was a stream that flowed into the low ground that was leveled by Jewish religious life" offers us a refreshed appreciation for the Jewish people.

I can only imagine what it must have been like, and still is to this day, to be continually persecuted for your faith, race and ethnicity at the same time, and to never have a sense that it is finally over. From the very beginning, Abraham to this day, the Jewish people have faced one holocaust after another and in so doing have provided a stepping stone for the Christian faith. All I can say is Wow!

Sanneh points out that the concept of the "end of the age" is Jewish; brought on by centuries of struggle and that Christianity developed with a focus on fulfillment and preparation for the end, the fulfillment of the journey. This is where mission began to touch the individual and create a personal responsibility for every Christian, and started separating from the Jewish corporate identity. Again, Sanneh's theme, standing together yet separate because Christianity was/is also strong in community, personal responsibility yet community minded. Here is where we find ourselves today, in the Twenty First Century, sometimes craving independence and sometimes longing for interdependence. Which does God desire, should we stand alone or stand in fellowship? Should we take care of our self, or should we depend on God?

The answer lies in our past, in the past is our beginning! Just as the pioneers of our faith trusted and depended on God, so too must we. Just as "God brought them out safe from their desperate circumstances", so too are we delivered. So regard not your situation today, no matter how difficult, just put your trust in God, the One who delivers!

My God and my King, thank you for bringing me the challenges of this life. As my strength fades, you are strong. Fill my life with your gentle presence, and when a reminder of your love is required, show me you are here. Today I pray for healing in my soul and body and the ability to serve you with bright and certain hope for tomorrow. In Jesus' Name I pray, AMEN!

***

Day 63

Dear brothers and sisters, when troubles come your way, consider it an opportunity for great joy. For you know that when your faith is tested, your endurance has a chance to grow. So let it grow, for when your endurance is fully developed, you will be perfect and complete, needing nothing. Jas 1:2-4 (NLT)

"By rising after my falls, and by frequently renewed acts of faith and love, I am come to a state wherein it would be as difficult for me not to think of God as it was at first to accustom myself to it." Brother Lawrence

Life will always be a challenge even though we are consistent in our longing for ease and carefree living. Why shouldn't we desire an easy life? Why shouldn't we understand Christ's words; "I will give you rest" as an invitation to leave the struggle behind and live in total comfort? Because, that is not what God has promised us. God has promised many things, if we are willing to accept His love, we will never be alone, we will be with Him for all eternity; we will have our needs provided for, and there are many more. IF, a little word with a big meaning, we accept God's love for us we will also accept all the promises of God because every promise of God is founded on His love.

There are three things God has never seen: God has never seen a person that has not sinned. (For all have sinned and fallen short of the glory of God. Rom 3:23) God has never seen a sinner He doesn't love. (For God so loved the world that he gave his one and only Son, that whoever believed in him should not perish but have eternal life. Jn 3:16) And third, God has never seen a sinner He cannot save. (For everyone who calls on the name of the Lord will be saved. Rom 10:13) JESUS LOVES ME THIS I KNOW!

Now, you decide: Which is the better life, an easy life, or a life lived with Christ at the heart of everything we do, and everywhere we go?

Dear LORD, I ask you to bring peace in the midst of war for our souls. My soul thirsts for refreshment today, and I know I am not alone as many seek comfort and a sense of your presence. So, in the name of the One and Only Christ, set my heart in a continual state of content as I know you are here. God, your forgiveness has made my life possible and your presence protects me from temptation every day. Thank you. In Christ I pray, AMEN!

***

Day 64

How we thank God for you! Because of you we have great joy as we enter God's presence. Night and day we pray earnestly for you, asking God to let us see you again to fill the gaps in your faith. May God our Father and our Lord make your love for one another and for all people grow and overflow, just as our love for you overflows. 1 Thess. 3:9-12 (NLT)

As a Christian, one always feels the tug at the heart to share this faith with others so they too may know the love of Christ. In our churches we preach the concept of mission and evangelizing the world and some people respond and travel to the ends of the earth to share the

Gospel. Still others respond and share with their next door neighbor and still other respond and live a dedicated life to the service of the Church. There are many ways to share the Gospel but the most important, and pivotal, way is the way we live our everyday life.

It is very easy to live life in America with a Western centric attitude, in other words, believing our way of worship and discipleship is the only way, or our music is the only style of true Christian music. And what about our worship style, have we not prejudged many on the way they worship? Worship wars have been raging in the American Church throughout its history. When the organ was introduced some cried heresy, when choirs began to sing some left the Church forever. When the Bible was finally available for average Christians to read the Church nearly crumbled. But in the meantime God has been doing something great.

During all these inner battles the Gospel has been infiltrating the world. When the first missionaries went to Ghana, in the nineteenth century, they packed their belongings in their own coffins. They knew they would not live to see the results of the Gospel being accepted. And more than 60% of them died there. In the 1880's Korea was a Christian vacuum, there were no Christian Churches in the whole country, but missionaries came and began introducing the Gospel. Today, South Korea is the second largest missionary sending country in the world! In Africa at the turn of the twentieth century, there were less than twelve million Christians. In 2010, on that continent, there are more than 495 million Christians and it is estimated to be over 1 billion by the year 2025!

Today, let's be thankful for the person(s) who first shared the Gospel with us, and let's be thankful for the many who have taken the Gospel to the world. And maybe, just maybe, we can follow in their footsteps!

Holy and Eternal God, bless all those who worship you today. May all praise be raised in honor of all you have created and sustained. Today I ask for your healing touch upon all who may be sick or injured and may all disease be banished in your name. O God, forgive the sins of our ignorance and selfishness and may this day be new and fresh, covered in your love and mercy. In Jesus' name, AMEN!

***

Day 65

The Lord is good and does what is right; he shows the proper path to those who go astray. He leads the humble in doing right, teaching them his way. The Lord leads with unfailing love and faithfulness all who keep his covenant and obey his demands. Ps 25:8-10 (NLT)

"That sounding bell dispels the waking dream, and tells me that I am still a wanderer." E.D. (19th century factory worker)

Where is God calling today? Where is God sending today? Who is God leading to today? Questions we must regularly ask ourselves because our Christian faith is never static, it is perpetually dynamic. But there is a problem, our human condition is such that rather than going, we are much more satisfied in staying put. We find our comfort zone and we want to stay there, protected from the outside world, walled off in total security.

In China there exists a perfect, tangible, example of this desire. It is called the Great Wall, vast and impressive, this monument to the human condition stands today after centuries of service to one purpose; keeping people out! This purpose was, and is, so important that portions of the wall wind through mountainous areas where no one could travel, let alone get over the wall. Yes, the mountains are impassable and yet the wall was still built, built to keep the people who could not even get to it, out! How ironic! But the wall has done its job, it has successfully isolated an entire nation from the rest of the world. Or has it?

Christians sometimes build their own great walls. We avoid people who do not share our belief and we isolate ourselves, not with a physical wall but with emotional and relational walls. Where is God calling? In our own neighborhoods there is crime, drug and alcohol addiction, abuse and depression. Where is God sending today? It is believed that 86% of all Muslims, Buddhists, and Hindus have never met a Christian. Who is God leading to today? Questions, questions that need answers! So pray for direction, pray for openings and opportunities to step out of your comfort zones and answer God call today.

Guiding Spirit of God, I ask you to lead me through this day with absolute confidence and proper direction. O God, help me see what you place before me; help me know you through all you speak, and help me love as you have loved me. I ask you to forgive my sins, today and yesterday, and lead me to a life lived without reservation, knowing that my mistakes, and sin, will always lead me to your mercy. And lastly, give me a measure of your mercy for all people, a full measure pressed down and overflowing. In Jesus' name, AMEN!

***

Day 66

Now we see a reflection in a mirror; then we will see face-to-face. Now I know partially, but then I will know completely in the same way that I have been completely known. Now faith, hope, and love remain – these three things – and the greatest of these is love. 1 Cor. 13:12-13 (CEB)

For each of us there is a place where we find love and acceptance, it may be with a group of friends but, hopefully, it is with our family. God's intentional emphasis on family serves as a model for community. But communities cannot be the model for family, the biblical model of family is the foundation for every community to function properly.

In the Old Testament, the Hebrew word for family meant "house" so when we say; "the household of God" we are referring to our familial relationship. The same Hebrew word is used for; "tribe" and "clan" so this word has more than just a nuclear family meaning, it has a general meaning of belonging. Like the old hymns sings; "I'm so glad I'm a part of the family of God, I've been washed in the fountain, cleansed by His blood. Joint heirs with Jesus as we travel this sod, I'm a part of the family, the family of God." Christian kinship is a blood relationship, it is a relationship based on common character made possible by the blood of Christ!

Being a family involves participating in a common tradition, sharing in a common character and a common destiny. This is the biblical vision of the household of God. Our common tradition begins with our obedience to God as we follow the commands handed down through the generations, to love God with all our, mind, strength and with all our heart, and to love our neighbor (community). Being the family of God means sharing in a common character, our example is Jesus Christ. Jesus lived a life of total devotion to God and to the people God loved, even when those people were evil toward him. How are we doing with the people who treat us poorly? And finally, as a part of the family of God, we share a common destiny which is eternal security through the sacrifice of Christ.

The Bible says, "Every house has a builder, but the builder behind them all is God. Moses did a good job in God's house, but it was all servant work, getting things ready for what was to come. Christ as Son is in charge of the house." (Heb. 3:5-6 MSSG) And, thanks be to God, we are all acceptable and invited into the household of God by the works of Christ and the Family of God.

LORD, in your mercy, hear my prayer; a prayer for wisdom to follow where you lead, courage to go where you send, and patience to await your divine will for our lives. O God, I ask for forgiveness to start this new day, and to accompany my spirit throughout, and I ask for healing and strength in my life, as well as, the lives of all in need of your touch today. In the awesome and loving name of Jesus Christ I pray, AMEN!

126

Day 67

Feed the hungry, and help those in trouble. Then your light will shine out of the darkness, and the darkness around you will be as bright as noon. The LORD will guide you continually, giving you water when you are dry and restoring your strength. You will be like a well-watered garden, like an ever flowing spring. Is 58:10-11 (NLT)

In the words of Jesus; "A city on a hill cannot hide its light..." But are we, the city, doing just that? When Christians avoid their identity in public we are hiding the Light of Christ, we are "hiding it under a bushel" instead of letting it shine for all to see. For example, when in the city, how many obvious homeless do we pass by? How many people do we see walking aimlessly on the sidewalks? At work, how many coworkers are suffering with difficulty in marriages, or with children and when they tell us about it we just nod our head and say, "that's tough?" Or, worse than all of these examples, there may be a family member, a brother, sister, or child whom we know is struggling with a major issue and, although concerned, we pray for them but never say "how can I help!"

We are justified in this one fact, WE cannot fix any of these situations, but God can! God can, and will enter into these situations but He needs our willingness to open the door. God has placed the Light within every believer for the purpose of providing the Light for others. Think about it, someone shared the Light with you and now you have the peace of knowing the darkness is overcome. Well God's plan is for you to share the Light you have with someone else. Don't worry, you can give away this Light every day and you will never be without it. That's the uniqueness of God's Light, the more you give away the more you have!

Here's your "double dog dare" for today, give away as much Light as you can, in every place you go, to every person you see, and I guarantee you will end the day with more Light than you started with! I double dog dare ya!

God of and for the ages; bring me continual hope today; hope for your world and for my life. Forgive and heal me with the strength of your hand and the wisdom of Your Holy Spirit. I pray for guidance and knowledge of your love as I praise Your Holy Name. AMEN!

***

Day 68

It is the LORD who created the stars, the Pleiades and Orion. He turns darkness into morning and day into night. He draws up water from the oceans and pours it down as rain on the land. The LORD is his name! Amos 5:8 (NLT)

When we begin our Christian life the problems of the world do not disappear. Disease still impacts our lives, either personally or someone we love gets sick. Life affects us all, some with diabetes, cancer, heart attacks, and maladies like Parkinson disease, these still happen. People we love, family members, still die and we experience the pain of separation. Even though the Christian has given complete control to God and accepted Christ into their heart, bad things still happen to these good people!

For example, when someone we love dies we often accuse God of taking them from us. I think this is an accusation we bring to God because we don't understand, usually when we are experiencing an acute pain in our life. And if that loss is the life of a child it magnifies the pain exponentially. But, let's see if together we can't make better sense of why God would allow things like this to happen. Why would God allow a child to lose his or her little life? From God's perspective that life is not lost. When God gives life He gives that life an eternal soul therefore, even when we think a child's life is lost God is able to restore to that child their life in heaven, so no loss is suffered on the part of the child. And in terms of eternal life, we will have the opportunity to be reunited one day, in heaven.

In the Bible, when David learned that the child he and Bathsheba had conceived died he said; "But why should I fast when he is dead? Can I bring him back again? I will go to him one day, but he cannot return to me." (2 Sam 12:23 NLT) This verse is God's assurance that the soul of infants is pure and belongs to God so life is not lost to the One who can restore it. So, what about the grief that parents and a family experience? In our loss, the presence of God is available to experience His strength, His comfort, His sustaining love and assurance in the face of the pain that exists. God sustains those who grieve for those He calls to Himself. The existence of any loss points to the reality of a God who can overcome even the worst things that happen.

Keep in mind, God does not take away, I know the Bible is often miss-quoted as saying the Lord gives and the Lord takes away, but the proper translation says;

"The Lord gives both death and life." (1 Sam 2:6) .God receives unto himself the souls of the pure in heart, and there is no more pure in heart than a child. This is why God considers us as His children. I know God does care for His children and knows the pain we often experience, we'd want no less a God. This is why many moms and dads who experience a miscarriage, a still born child, or even after seeing the mistake of an abortion give their child a name and celebrate the brief impact that tiny life made upon their lives.

The point is this; there are no easy answers for our losses, nothing to instantly take the pain away. But I do know that God loves us and most assuredly all those who now rest in His arms. My hope is that we will find the comfort of His presence breaking through the hurt to reveal the love of His Son Jesus right where we are.

From the rising of the sun to the setting, all honor and praise is yours, O God. You have blessed my life with your love and acceptance, and I pray for the needs and desires of all your children, from infant to adult, that they may be blessed as I am blessed. As I seek your forgiveness help me to forgive others and may my life be a true and certain testimony to Your Holy Spirit. In the loving name of Jesus Christ, AMEN!

***

Day 69

He went on a little farther and bowed his face to the ground, praying. "My Father! If it is possible, let this cup of suffering be taken away from me, yet I want your will to be done, not mine."—"My Father! If this cup cannot be taken away unless I drink it, your will be done." Matt 26:39,42 (NLT)

"Courage is being scared to death and saddling up anyway!" John Wayne

How often are we tempted to keep to ourselves and worry only about what "I" need? Becoming self-centered does not happen, the reality is that we are born with an inner need to be concerned with self! The moment we come into this world we begin to learn how to get what we want. You may not have a specific memory of this, but when you first felt hunger, when your tiny stomach began to fire the synapse connections in your brain that screamed out "FEED ME", you responded with all the strength you could muster. And you cried out as loud as you could until someone responded and fed you. And suddenly you just learned your first life lesson. Yes, you learned that when you want something for yourself all you have to do is cry, and it worked every time.

In the business world this philosophy is alive and well. Sayings like; "The squeaky wheel gets the grease!" and; "If it is to be, it is up to me!" prove we have learned our lessons well. Conversely we have also learned how to protect ourselves by avoiding potentially dangerous experiences that would jeopardize the situation. This is true especially with topics in life that will render us vulnerable to the attack of failure. Sharing our Christian faith is sometimes one of the most threatening of these possibilities. We wonder, maybe I will be rejected, maybe I will be ridiculed and teased, maybe I will offend and they will begin avoiding me, maybe I'll say the wrong thing and make a fool of myself! There is a key word in every one of these fears; MAYBE.

Jesus said; "...don't worry about how to respond or what to say. God will give you the right words at the right time." (Matt 10:19 NLT) He didn't say maybe or even sometimes, Jesus said "God will..." that's a promise friend. So, rather than worrying about the potential negative consequences of sharing our Christian witness perhaps we should worry about the real consequences of not sharing. Look for opportunities today to share the love Christ has shared with you, God will give you the words.

LORD, you save me every day. I seek your forgiveness and direction as I set out on the day's journey, knowing no matter what I face; danger or challenge, you are with me. Let me see you today, in every face, in every situation and in every place I go. For you are the King of the universe, AMEN!

***

Day 70

You can enter God's Kingdom only through the narrow gate. The highway to hell is broad, and its gate is wide for the many who choose that way. But the gateway to life is very narrow and the road is difficult, and only a few ever find it. Matt 7:13-14

"In all the day long as at the appointed times of prayer; for at all times, every hour, every minute, even in the height of my business, I drove away from my mind everything that was capable of interrupting my thought of God." Brother Lawrence

What was your last thought before drifting off the sleep last night? What was your first thought when you awoke this morning? Many times both are either the same, or very closely related. This is why, in the formative years of our faith, we read so much about times of prayer. Jesus frequently went away to a quiet place to pray, both evening and morning. Sometimes so early in the morning that the sun had not yet come up, and sometime so late at night that his disciples could not stay awake. There's a lesson there for us.

I believe the thee most important ingredients for effective prayers are spelled out for us in 1 Corinthians 13, commonly known as "The Love Chapter". I know, we usually think that this is speaking about a relationship, that's why we use chapter 13 in so many weddings. But think in context of prayer. Prayer without; faith, hope, and love is empty prayer. Without faith prayer is futile, there is no direction to prayer, it becomes just words spoken. Without hope there is no point to prayer, no divine element to prayer and no joy in prayer. And with love, well without love there is no one listening to our prayer making the whole exercise pointless.

Tonight, before you drift off to sleep simply say a prayer of thanks to God for all the things you have and the people you love. Tomorrow, see if you don't awaken to thoughts of joy and gratitude.

Jesus, blessed Redeemer, Loving Spirit, Creator of all that is and is to come; my eyes are turned to you, this day and every day. Forgive my sins, turn me from selfish practice, and guide me to the life path you have chosen. Cleanse my thoughts so my prayer will be pure and certain, and hear this prayer for all your children today as you fill their hearts with love, joy and peace. In Jesus' name, AMEN!

***

Day 71

When he heard this, Jesus said, "This illness isn't fatal. It's for the glory of God so that God's Son can be glorified through it." ... When he heard Lazarus was ill, he stayed where he was. After two days, he said to his disciples, "Let's return to Judea again." Jn 11:4,6-7 (CEB)

All too often we find ourselves relying on what we can accomplish for Christ. We work to perfect our strengths and gifts of grace so WE can do great things for the Kingdom. Education, spiritual development, mission experience and resources for ministry are all good things to pursue but the reality is, our own strength and talent is not what will get the Kingdom work done.

Philippians 4:13 reads; "For I can do everything through Christ, who gives me strength." And the opposite is also true; I can do nothing without Christ, for I am weak! Here's the point, we must always rely on God's ability to do things through us, not our ability to do things for God. It is the work of the Holy Spirit that frees us and empowers us to do the work of the Kingdom. Where would David have found the strength to defeat Goliath were it not for God? Where would Noah have found the motivation to build the Ark if God had not spoken to him? How would Moses have communicated the direction of freedom to the Israelites if God had not given him the words and the assistance of Aaron?

Yes, Christians do good things, but even good things can be not so good if they are done in any other name but God's. So allow God to complete the work of your hands today as you follow His lead and answer His call to change the world around you.

Great and Almighty God, my prayer today is for the patience of Christ and the faith to match. Make my life a life of testimony to your sovereign grace. Forgive my sin, yesterday and today, and may my life testify to the world that I am forgiven, complete and whole. This I pray through Christ, who strengthens me. AMEN!

***

Day 72

We put our hope in the LORD. He is our help and our shield. In him our hearts rejoice, for we trust in his holy name. Let your unfailing love surround us, LORD, for our hope is in you alone. Ps 33:20-22 (NLT)

Many people wear glasses to help them see clearly, some from a very young age and others find their sight changing as they grow older. Some people need glasses due to myopathy, others simply for magnification to help in reading. There are many levels of sight that require the use of glasses. But there is one set of glasses that every Christian needs to use, let's call them "Grace Glasses."

Imagine seeing a future of total redemption through God's love, a world filled with peace, kindness and understanding, a world led by grace rather than judgment. Well, to help bring out a new future, a new creation, that is a world we can only see through grace glasses! When we put on grace glasses we will see our true selves and how much we need God's help in everyday life. We will see the needs of our families, our neighbors and friends, as well as the needs across the world. Grace glasses help us see the people who are estranged from God, co-workers, the person who waited on you at the store, the alcoholic in front of the Bar, and we won't turn our heads we will take time to help introduce God into their life!

Grace glasses allow us to see with God's eyes, and when we do this we are deciphering the image with our heart, not with our brain. We are discerning God's will with grace glasses, not making decision for self-preservation. When we see through grace glasses we are called to the mission of helping, one person at a time, and to introduce the God of love and grace. Our mission is not motivated by success, our motivation is simply the grace with which God looks at us as redemption became a possibility, and out of gratitude for God's great love for us, we are compelled to share with others.

Today, maybe you have a neighbor struggling with a rebellious child, or you have a friend whose marriage is near crumbling, or you have someone near you battling addiction, or you know a place in the city where the homeless are staying, or you know someone who is dealing with cancer, or you are aware of a family grieving the death of a loved one and you see them, but when you see them through grace glasses you know you must go to them and help. Can you see clearly?

God, your presence is evident in the entire world, in the trees and leaves, in the sounds of the birds, in the coolness of the morning breeze and in the warmth of the afternoon sun. May the blessing of creation touch every heart today, and may your unfailing love and forgiveness cover every life. And, LORD, today I dedicate my life to you once more: In the name of the Risen Christ. AMEN!

***

Day 73

Dear friends, I am not writing a new commandment for you; rather it is an old one you have had from the beginning. This old commandment—to love one another—is the same message you heard before. Yet it is also new. Jesus lived the truth of this commandment, and you also are living it. For the darkness is disappearing, and the true light is already shining. 1 Jn 2:7-8 (NLT)

"Sometimes I consider myself there as a stone before a carver, whereof he is to make a statue; presenting myself thus before God, I desire him to form His perfect image in my soul, and make me entirely like Himself." Brother Lawrence

There is a beautiful chorus in which we sing; "Spirit of the Living God, fall afresh on me. Spirit of the Living God, fall afresh on me. Melt me, mold me, fill me, use me. Spirit of the Living God, fall afresh on me. You are the potter, I am the clay, melt me and mold me, this is what I pray. Spirit of the Living God, fall afresh on me." The message of these words is one of submission and willingness to surrender to God's sovereignty.

The Christian faith is cross formed and resurrection shaped. Because the cross is an instrument of death it symbolizes an end to the former life. The selfish ways cease and the life lived oblivious to any higher being comes to an end when we accept the sacrifice of Christ. The cross did that for each of us, without reservation, making known to us a love so perfect it encompasses all of creation. Yes, the cross has formed the Christian faith, but the cross is only the beginning, once formed there is a new journey. The former life is passed away and a new life begins, resurrection now becomes the center of a Christian life.

Resurrection shapes every aspect of Christian life. Christ, resurrected from the dead, did not immediately ascend to heaven; there remained further work to be done. In a period of forty days, as we are told by Scripture, Christ appeared before many believers. In these meetings spiritual lives were shaped into resurrection powered, and centered, servants. Each experience with the resurrected Christ led to the beginning of an apostolic mission and the movement we call the Church began. The concept of resurrection, the second chance, became the factor upon which salvation was preached and shared with others which was followed by the logical conclusion that God loves all His creation.

Our lives as Christians are shaped, carved, molded, and polished everyday through the resurrection. Christ died for you, Christ rose for you, and Christ lives for you!

Precious LORD, take my hand, lead me to your promised land. As I wait your directions for this day, O God, know that my love for you, though not capable of equaling your love for me, is yet growing. I forgive all others today, as you forgive me, and I seek your will only as I journey through this life toward complete and total communion in you. In Christ I pray, AMEN!

***

Day 74

I thank Christ Jesus our Lord, who has given me strength to do his work. He considered me trustworthy and appointed me to serve him, even though I used to blaspheme the name of Christ. In my insolence, I persecuted his people. But God had mercy on me because I did it in ignorance and unbelief. Oh, how generous and gracious our Lord was! He filled me with the faith and love that come from Christ Jesus. 1 Tim 1:12-14 (NLT)

Sometimes it is useful to glance in the rearview mirror, glance but not stare. If we find ourselves starring in the rearview mirror we forget where we are steering and, well, you know what happens then… Throughout our lives we receive many well wished pieces of advice, one of which is a saying such as, "Always remember where you have come from." a sage and valuable saying indeed. I believe such a saying is a directive to take an occasional glance in the rearview mirror.

Take a moment and glance in that mirror, see where you have been. But always give greater attention to where you are going for Christ. A glance in the rearview mirror can remind us of what life was like before, before the blessings we enjoy today, relationships, marriage, children, grandchildren, a job, a home, a church home, etc. you get the rearview picture. But the most relevant thing we can see in this memory glance is that all the things we enjoy as blessings from the hand of God have all been made possible because we accepted Christ as Lord and Savior of our life.

Before making that decision you are faced with today, take a glance in the mirror for a reminder of decisions made without Christ, reflect on how things worked out. Before giving that word of advice to a family member or a friend, take a glance back and remember how your advice was shaped before Christ. Before every prayer you offer to God today, take a glance and remember what your prayer life was before Christ. My guess is, you will see a clear difference in everything you do today when you remember how your life was before Christ, and you will feel the warmth of His love knowing you will never be the same again.

Holy and Loving Christ: You have blessed me beyond my greatest dreams. Today I give you thanks for the work you have blessed me with, for family to love and for all your children. Thank you for giving me voice with which to speak of your magnificent works, and hands with which to reach out to others. Thank you for cleansing my soul with forgiveness, and impressing upon me my duty to forgive all others. In the name of my blessed Savior, Jesus Christ, AMEN!

***

Day 75

What joy comes for those whose strength comes from the LORD, who have set their minds on a pilgrimage to Jerusalem. When they walk through the Valley of Weeping, it will become a place of refreshing springs. The autumn rains will clothe it with blessings. They will continue to grow stronger, and each of them will appear before God in Jerusalem. Ps 84:5-7 (NLT)

Mother Teresa said many noteworthy sayings, but one that has always impressed me is her words about forgiving people. Remember, Mother Teresa intentionally went to the sick, the lepers, the AIDS patients who no one else wanted to go near. She held them, she hugged them and yes, she kissed them no matter how unclean and detestable they appeared. Mother Teresa humbly understood that the greatest disease the world has to combat is not a physical malady, or even a psychological or emotional one, she knew the greatest disease the world faces is the inability to forgive. She said; "People are often unreasonable and self-centered. Forgive them anyway!"

Christ, when on the cross, looked up to heaven and said; "Father forgive them for they do not know what they are doing!" (Lk 23:34) That one short prayer may just be the one that has made the greatest difference in my, as well as your, life. The prayer Christ offered for us has been a shield, a hedge of protection around us as we continue to exist in our ignorance, always providing an open door for us to walk into greater understanding. And we come to know that this journey or pilgrimage as we sometimes call it; is one fraught with challenge and danger. We risk falling back into our old ways every day, because we do not know all the answers.

If you have ever happened upon a deer in the woods, or any wild animal for that matter, you have seen their reaction to your human invasion of their space. The wild animal in most cases will choose flight over fight and they will run back in the direction they came from, because that is familiar territory and they know it was safer than staying, or continuing in the same direction. We, like the deer in the woods, many times choose to retreat in the direction we came from because we know what was there and we fear what may be ahead, choosing to condemn others, or avoid them, rather than forgive. Forgiving is new territory, we don't know what's ahead and we feel the instability of the unknown. On the other hand if we condemn it may be our escape. Get the picture?

Christ chooses to forgive, not directing what our response will be but trusting us to make the decision. Yes, God is disappointed many times, but God never stops loving and never stops forgiving. Can you say "Thanks?"

Heavenly Father; I thank you for providing all that I need; you give me peace, comfort and healing. I set my eyes on you for your grace is the source of understanding and acceptance. You reach down to the pit of my despair and give me confidence and joy. Now, I give back to you by offering every gift you have given me to your children. I pray this in your full and beautiful name; Father, Son and Holy Spirit. AMEN!

***

Day 76

(Jesus Prayed) Just as you sent me into the world, I am sending them into the world. And I give myself as a holy sacrifice for them so they can be made holy by your truth. I am praying not only for these disciples but also for all who will ever believe in me through their message.   Jn 17:18-20 (NLT)

"We have a God who is infinitely gracious and knows all our wants." Brother Lawrence

Sometimes it seems the world around us has fallen to pieces. For example; exactly one year before writing this note to you, on this very date, I was preparing for surgery. In fact, I read the same Scripture, John 17:18-20 and I prayed the same prayer here written below. My ordered world was soon to be disheveled and torn to pieces. Before me, beginning this very day lay a long road to recovery and the unknown effects of cancer. The doctors had prepared me for the worst and rightfully so, but there was something that whispered peace in my ear. My family was gathered around me, and the family of God was praying for me and holding me before the throne of God. I found myself remembering a story I had read, years before, about a little boy who found himself very bored one winter day and how he taught his mother the value of family.

It was a cold day and playing outside was not a possibility, the little boy tried to find things to do inside,

143

but with no one to play with, boredom soon took over. He went to his mother and asked; "Mommy, what can I do, I'm bored." Well his mother suggested several things, each met with; "No, I don't want to…" Finally his mother had an idea, she would make a puzzle for him to put together, hoping that it would occupy him for at least an hour. So she took a magazine and on the back page there was a full page picture of the world. She proceeded to cut the page into dozens of pieces, then placed them on the table and mixed and tossed them into one pile of unrecognizable chaos and handed the boy some scotch tape.

"There," she said to her son, "now put the puzzle back together."

The little boy went to work, carefully looking over the pieces, front and back, shape by shape. The mother went about her work and left him thinking she would not hear from him for some time. Then, just a few minutes later she heard; "MOM!" And she went into the kitchen to see what her son needed, thinking he was confused and stumped.

"I'm finished," he said, "come and see."

The mother walked into the kitchen, sure enough the boy had completed the puzzle. She was amazed and asked, "How in the world did you do that so quickly?"

"Easy," he said, "I just put the picture of the family together on the back of the page and the world was in one piece!"

That day, one year before this writing, my world was in one piece, and one PEACE, because God had blessed me with a family. My genetic family and my spiritual family were, and remain, one family under God and I am truly blessed. I trust you too can sense God's blessing in the same way.

My heart is filled with praise, for you Oh God. In the stillness of the morning I hear your voice and feel your gentle breath, make me an instrument of your peace today, continue to restore me through your healing touch so I may serve you. Bless all who have been blessings to me and give them strength of heart, mind, body and soul. All this I pray in the name of the One, Only, Messiah, Christ, AMEN!

***

Day 77

Peter replied, "Change your hearts and lives. Each of you must be baptized in the name of Jesus Christ for the forgiveness of your sins. Then you will receive the gift of the Holy Spirit." Acts 2:38 (NLT)

"We must, nevertheless, always work at it, because not to advance in the spiritual life is to go back." Brother Lawrence

Believe it or not, our life today is a product of nurture, as well as nature. The debate has raged as to which has a greater impact on our personality and behavior but suffice to say, both nature and nurture play a role. The ways we respond to people in need are closely shaped by the ways we observed adults when we were young. In some, I said some, cases a child will develop habits exactly as observed, but the opposite is also true. For example; two siblings, a brother and a sister grew up in the home of alcoholic parents. As adults one is an alcoholic and the other is a "tea-totaler" who has never touched alcohol. When asked: "Why did you become what you are today?" Both the brother and the sister will give you the same answer; "If you grew up in the home I did, you would be this way too." One outcome is good, the other tragic but both products of the same raw material. The point is, the tragic life of the one gripped by alcohol could have been prevented.

The nurture we receive affects our future lives, and the lives of others. Even in terms of helping the poor the sick and the lonely. Another example; a little boy has a birthday party and he opens a card from his grandmother, inside is a crisp dollar bill. He is asked: "Are you going to use part of it to help the poor?"

"No," he replies, "I'm going to buy some candy and the store owner can use it to help the poor, if he wants to." Amusing, but again, a tragic outcome due to the way the child was nurtured. Too often we show children that someone else will help, not us. Again, the risk is too great to leave to chance. We are called to model Christ-like behavior to all children so when Christ says; "That which you did for the least of these..." (Matt 25) we will be blessed. Now, go do the right thing today!

God of the morning, noon and night; today is a day for growth in Your Spirit. I pray for progress and continued strength. I ask you for a blessing, not for me alone but, for all who worship you today. I pray for healing for all who love you and follow you. I pray for forgiveness for mine and all the sins of all your children today, and may Your Spirit be the light that guides me and the source of all my strength. In the Name of Christ, my LORD, AMEN!

***

Day 78

Therefore, since we are surrounded by such a huge crowd of witnesses to the life of faith, let us strip off every weight that slows us down, especially the sin that so easily trips us up. And let us run with endurance the race God has set before us. Heb. 12:1 (NLT)

"When we covet what our neighbor has we say to Almighty God; 'You haven't been fair!'" Dr David Jeremiah

Wanting more and more and more seems to be common in the world today. Political leaders want more influence, dictators want more control, and capitalists want more money. Even churches sometimes want more, but the goal is to want more in a healthy way. The healthy way of wanting more is the way that benefits God's Kingdom, not a personal gain for a person or a people. When the Israelites left Egypt they lived for forty years, as they wandered in the wilderness, trying to find what they needed.

At one point, at a place called Meribah which means unfaithfulness, the people called out to Moses demanding they be taken back to Egypt where they had everything they needed to survive. But in Egypt they may have had food for their bodies but no food for their souls. Their values were warped, their thinking had been turned inward and all they wanted was to be comfortable, fat and happy. Unfortunately all was at the expense of their spiritual health. Only after forty years did they finally come to the point in their journey when they gave all their faith to God and they entered into the Promised Land against overwhelming odds in order to receive what God had promised. A healthy desire for more of God in their lives and society finally took root. The Temple was built and the Synagogue system was developed and God became the center of their lives and communities.

For today, in the Church, wanting more is only acceptable and healthy when we want more for the Kingdom of God. We can healthily want more people whose lives are drawn to Christ, we can want better buildings for the purpose of teaching God's ways, we can want more financial resources, provided we are using every penny for the fulfillment of the Gospel. In short, Christians are to want more opportunities to fulfill the Great Commission, "make disciples", and the Great Commandments, "Love God and Love the people God loves", so that God is first in every heart. Go ahead, ask for more!

Holy and Eternal God, You have provided all I need to live and thrive and I thank you. Grow within my heart a strong desire to follow you, even into places I would not go alone. Allow my spirit to welcome Your Spirit and may my life always seek your direction. By your grace make me whole again so I may serve you with energy and zeal and bless all who serve and worship you this day, in the fullness of Your Word and presence. All of this I pray in the wonderful name of Jesus Christ, my LORD and Savior. AMEN!

***

Day 79

The same Good News that came to you is going out all over the world. It is bearing fruit everywhere by changing lives, just as it changed your lives from the day you first heard and understood the truth about God's wonderful grace. Col. 1:6 (NLT)

"If you seek it by faith, you may expect it as you are: and if you are, then expect it now." John Wesley (Sermon 43 – 1765)

The Good News, the truth of the Gospel of Jesus Christ, has come to each Christian in a powerful and unique way. Some have listened and feasted on the Word since infancy and their personality was shaped and nurtured in Christ all their lives. They know no other way to live but in Christ. Others may have experienced the same upbringing but rebelled at a later date. Their lives were also shaped and nurtured albeit by their own hand, leading them down dangerous paths, narrowly avoiding events that could lead to death and eternal condemnation. In fact, some did not avoid this tragic outcome. Still others are fortunate enough to find their way home, as the Prodigal in Luke 15, who was raised in a faithful home and yet the world's temptations drew him away. But when he hit bottom he returned home.

The point is, there are many paths our lives may go down, by our decisions and choices. However, there is but one way to salvation. "You are saved through faith." (Eph. 2:8) is a short but powerful statement from God. Saved, or salvation, as it is commonly referred to has been widely misunderstood throughout Christian history. The popular notion of salvation is focused on a location, or a destination, heaven. But the reality, based on the Word of God, is that salvation is now! The very moment we decide to surrender our heart to God, to allow Jesus Christ to become the Lord of our life, we experience salvation. As Wesley said; "then expect it now." now because you have faith in God, the Almighty who has promised to save you. Expect it now because salvation is God's entire work, from the beginning of creation, from the dawning of grace in the soul until it is consummated in glory, God is at work for the purpose of our salvation. This is why, when anyone chooses to turn and run toward home, or anyone lives a devoted life and professes Jesus Christ as Lord, salvation in real to them.

Have you any doubt you stand forgiven and saved? Have you doubt that someone you know can have it? Well, rest assured, as Paul writes; "If you confess with your mouth that Jesus is Lord and believe in your heart that God raised him from the dead, you will be saved." (Rom 10:9 NLT) So, expect it NOW!

Dear God; Yours the last name and person my thoughts turned to at the end of the day, also the first in the freshness of the morning. Thank you for providing all that I need and thank you for reminding me what my needs are. My need for forgiveness in the midst of my sinful ways, my need for strength in times of weakness, my need for healing in times of brokenness and my need for companionship in the midst of loneliness. To You, O God I dedicate my life and I will follow you where you lead, and I will go where you send me. In the name of Jesus Christ I raise this prayer. AMEN!

***

Day 80

But when you pray, go away by yourself, shut the door behind you, and pray to your Father in private. Then your Father, who sees everything, will reward you. When you pray, don't babble on and on as people of other religions do. They think their prayers are answered merely by repeating their words again and again. Don't be like them, for your Father knows exactly what you need even before you ask him! Matt 6:6-8 (NLT)

"There is not in the world a kind of life more sweet and delightful than that of a continual conversation with God." Brother Lawrence

Prayer is conversation with God. When asked to pray in public many Christians politely pass because there is tremendous anxiety and questions about what to say and how to say it. Other Christians leap at the opportunity and launch into a holy voice led by pious words and long extraneous sentences filled with words like Thee and Thou and Thus! But what really pleases God, in my opinion, is nothing more than having a talk with one He loves.

When Jesus said, "go away by yourself," he did not mean that literally even though going away to a private place is a good experience and he did that many times. In this context he is speaking of everyday prayer, as we would pray at the table, or for a sick friend, or yes even if we were asked to pray in public as at the beginning or end of a meeting with other Christians. Going away by yourself, in this instance, means step away from the crowd and talk with God as if it is just the two of you in the room, have a conversation.

Think about how you talk with a friend, talking about the weather for example. Well, this friend, God, is the One you can thank for the weather, or ask for better weather. When you talk with a friend you talk of subjects you have in common, sports, crafts, hobbies etc. Well, one huge thing we have in common with God is our need for forgiveness; we sin and God forgives, why not talk about that with God?

I remember my grandfather telling the story about my younger cousin and how, when he asked him to pray before dinner one day, simply prayed; "Lord, thanks for the food but I'm so hungry that's all I want to say! Amen!" You know something? That short prayer from the lips of a child probably said more to a loving Heavenly Father than the longest eloquent waxes from any profession clergy person in the world! Simply stated, a short honest, genuine prayer is a great conversation between child and Heavenly Father: Amen? You just prayed!

Hello LORD! I love to walk with you during the day, and rest in your arms through the night. I pray that all your children, from every land and every faith, will also continue in your presence. I always give thanks to you for the many folk who have assisted you in changing my life and helping me hold out my hand to yours. And I thank you for forgiving my sins, those of yesterday and today. And Lord, I pledge to forgive also, in your beautiful Name. AMEN!

***

Day 81

My brothers and sisters, think of the various tests you encounter as occasions for joy. After all, you know that the testing of your faith produces endurance. Let this endurance complete its work so that you may be fully mature, complete, and lacking in nothing. Jas 1:2-4 (CEB)

"The Law of happiness: Happy people are grateful people, and grateful people are happy people!" Henry Cloud

When a marathon runner comes to the starting line it is hardly the beginning. Months, and years, of preparation and practice have preceded this. Rising early in the morning and running many miles, on a daily basis, in order to train the muscles in the body, to strengthen, and to condition for the purpose of this very day so that every possible opportunity to perform at the peak of efficiency exists. When a musician performs before a crowd, in concert, the music that pleases every ear and heart is a result of many hours over years of preparation and practice. The product of these many hours is the near perfect performance that brings the audience to their feet in applause when finished. When the student sits down at a desk and is handed an exam packet and takes pencil in hand, it is after months of reading, study and listening in order to learn the information for which the test measures their understanding.

In every race, performance, and academic endeavor there is only one goal, and that is the goal of accomplishment. To know that the reward for all the hard work and perseverance paid off is to know that each day was worth the struggle. The Apostle Paul wrote; "I will be proud that I did not run the race in vain and that my work was not useless." (Phil 2:16 NLT) notice Paul separates the race from the work. Every day, as a child of God, there is work to do in preparation, training and practice for the big event. What will that event be? Will it be the test of our will in the face of temptation? Will it be the test of our faith when receiving a difficult diagnosis? Will it be the challenges of observing our son or daughter make a bad choice? Will it be the tragic loss of a life of a loved one? Will it be facing extreme disappointment of failure, either financially or of a relationship?

The reality is that all of these challenges are possible, and there are many other possibilities. Jesus said; "Here on this earth you will have many trials and sorrows. But take heart, because I have overcome the world." (Jn 16:33 NLT) but Jesus also showed us how to overcome the trials and sorrows. It boils down to how we practice our faith, how we approach our training process and develop our spiritual skills through prayer, meditating on the Scripture, and trusting God with the things beyond our abilities. When we know in our heart that God is our security we find happiness, and joy beyond our personal abilities.

New every morning is your love, O God of the universe. My praise for you is unending and my desire to serve you has no end, so I ask for your forgiveness and a clean slate for this day, but not just an easing of my sins, I also ask for awareness of my sins so I will not repeat them. I ask You LORD, to heal all who need your touch today. Give strength to the weak and power to the oppressed. And, may Your Spirit be the presence within mine, and all lives today! In the Name of the Father, the Son, and the Holy Spirit I pray. AMEN!

***

Day 82

And so dear brothers and sisters, I plead with you to give your bodies to God because of all he has done for you. Let them be a living and holy sacrifice – the kind he will find acceptable. This is truly the way to worship him. Rom 12:1 (NLT)

"The only problem we have with being a holy and living sacrifice is, we squirm off the altar!" Rick Warren

Have you ever stopped to think; where would I be without God? Even someone who is not a dedicated disciple of Christ should consider life without God. First, Christians believe God has created all things and therefore, without God we would not be here. Without God; the rain would not fall, the flowers would not bloom, and winds would not blow. Without God; humanity would have no model for relationships, we would be no different than any other mammal on earth and survival of the fittest would be the norm.

Without God we would also have no model for behavior. Think of the things that we do because God did them first; the ability to know right from wrong, understanding, empathy, sympathy, forgiveness, and love are all original ideas of God handed to us. And let us never forget faith; faith begins with God's faith in us. We are afforded the gift of free-will which proves God has faith in us, God trusts us to make the choices in life that will affect our eternal security and also impact the eternal security of others. This is why Paul says; "I plead with you to give your bodies to God because of all he has done for you." Paul had experienced, first hand, the changing presence of God in his life.

Where would you be without God today? Where are you with God today? These are two questions Christians need to ask regularly so we can objectively and critically examine our worthy sacrifice we offer to God.

Gracious and Heavenly God, through your work in my life, I am made complete. I ask for your continued companionship and forgiveness. I ask for your special attention to everyone who struggles today, with sickness, injury or disease of any kind. Make your call loud and clear today and send me to doing the work you have called me to. In Jesus' name; AMEN!

***

Day 83

Then the LORD said to me, "Write my answer plainly on tablets, so that a runner can carry the correct message to others. This vision is for a future time. It describes the end, and it will be fulfilled. If it seems slow in coming, wait patiently, for it will surely take place. It will not be delayed." Hab. 2:2-3 (NLT)

"…we must serve God in a holy freedom; we must do our business faithfully, without trouble or disquiet, recalling our mind to God mildly, and with tranquility,.." Brother Lawrence

Have you ever walked into a room to get something and stopped, scratched your head and thought; "What did I come in here to get?" Many times we Christians become so busy with the everyday responsibilities of life we forget what we are here for! It's easy to fall into this trap but when we become so wrapped up in our walled existence, people who need to know Christ suffer.

Mark Gornic, in his book "To Live in Peace" writes about a young boy who grew up in Baltimore's inner city. As an African American he faced many prejudices and stereotypes. His name was Rodney, he excelled in school but dropped out after the eighth grade. His father had left the family alone shortly before and his mother worked two jobs to support the family. Rodney had tremendous potential, but he never met Jesus, no one ever shared with him how God valued him. When Rodney was eighteen years old his lifeless body was found in an abandoned row house in the Sandtown area of Baltimore. Rodney had been murdered in an apparent drug deal gone bad, like so many other young men in the city. Rodney's death was a tragedy that could have been avoided, if only someone had introduced him to Jesus.

As Christians we rarely consider how many lives we could save by sharing Jesus Christ. Jesus said; "You are the salt of the earth...You are the light of the world...the yeast a woman used in making the bread..." (Matt 5:13, Lk 13:21 NLT) Our roll is to share everything about Jesus Christ so that the world may know, and the Rodney's of the world will have a better reason to live. Perhaps, just maybe, the efforts we put forth in telling others about Christ may save some lives. May the Peace of Christ be our motivation today!

LORD, your nature overwhelms me, you are forgiving in all things, loving in every way, and understanding of my every thought. While you do not look away from disobedience but have set in motion the consequences for every action, I stand convicted of your sovereignty today. I pray your healing presence in my life today, as well as, in every believer. In Your Name, Christ, I pray. AMEN!

***

Day 84

One Sabbath day Jesus was teaching in the synagogue, he saw a woman who had been crippled by an evil spirit. She had been bent double for eighteen years and was unable to stand up straight. When Jesus saw her he called her over and said, "Dear woman, you are healed of your sickness!" Then he touched her, and instantly she could stand straight. How she praised God! Lk 13:10-14 (NLT)

Today's decisions will make tomorrow's memories. Some decisions are good and positive and lead to pleasant memories, the things we return to when we struggle; some call them the "good old" days', the times when we were happy. Good decisions make good memories. But in life we do not always make good decisions; sometimes our decisions are bad decisions. Bad decisions make bad memories, the experiences we would much rather avoid repeating. Bad memories can either cripple our progress or enable our progress by serving as wisdom for future decisions.

158

There is an old south western story about being confronted with the choice between a good and a bad decision. It's about a water well in the middle of the desert, an old style hand pump well. On the handle was hanging a bucket full of water with a small sign on it. The sign read; "This here bucket-o-water is fer primin this here pump so ya'll ken pump some water. Dump the whole bucket down er to prime er and be sure ta fill the bucket after yer done drinkin so the next feller ken prime er".

Whoever came across that well and read the sign is suddenly faced with a decision. The first thought, after walking through the dry parched desert, is to immediately drink the water from the bucket. The fear is: what if the whole bucket is dumped down the well and the pump doesn't prime? The result of a decision to disregard the advice of the sign would be a temporary quenching of thirst but a lifetime of regret, wondering how many people came to the well after that moment and found no water to prime the pump. A bad decision makes a bad memory.

But a decision to accept the advice, in faith, is a decision made for all future desert travelers. One that is rewarded with more than one bucket of water, a decision rewarded with good memories of having helped many other weary hikers find a refreshing drink of water; a good memory indeed. Others before you and me have had faith enough to prime the well of salvation and we have been blessed. The question for today is, will I prime the pump, or will I use the water for myself?

My heart fills with Praise for you, Great God of the universe! Even in times when I feel set back, you triumph. On days when all seems to be difficult and filled with pain, your soothing balm of love and forgiveness restores me. All praise in heaven and on earth is yours, Great and Almighty God. AMEN!

***

Day 85

In the beginning God created the heavens and the earth. The earth was formless and empty, and darkness covered the deep waters. And the Spirit of God was hovering over the surface of the waters. Then God said, "Let there be light," and there was light. And God saw that the light was good. Then he separated the light from the darkness. God called the light "day" and the darkness "night." Gen 1:1-5 (NLT)

In many ways humanity is foreign to the created world. We have minds that distinguish between right and wrong, not brains that make decisions only for survival. We have a spiritual existence that, for some, becomes the catalyst for decision making. And we have been blessed with the freedom of choice which allows us the privilege of relationships with all of God's creation. One would think humanity would automatically have it all together, or as the popular rap saying goes; "auto-magically" have it together. Not true, because of free choice the reality is, we sometimes make the wrong choice! This is why today's Christian missionaries are trained in decision making before entering a new culture.

Missionaries are trained that there is a dichotomy they need to understand when going into a new culture. They are trained to know that their experience, positive

160

or negative, will depend on where their attitude begins. There are two options, the attitude toward the new culture may be one of; fear, suspicion and inflexibility. The other option is the Christian option; an attitude of openness, acceptance and trust. When the cultural differences are experienced the reaction is based on the beginning attitude; fear, suspicion and inflexibility cause criticism, rationalization and withdrawal leading to alienation and isolation. That means the mission fails.

However, when differences are experienced from the Christian foundation of openness, acceptance and trust the cultural differences cause observation, listening and inquiring leading to rapport and understanding. Now the mission begins to thrive. This is what God created humanity to be, in fruitful relationship with one another, and with all of creation. The positive approach is just as easy as the negative, requiring the same amount of effort. It all starts with our beginning attitude.

People do have differences, true, but people also have one major thing in common, a loving Heavenly Father who has created all. So seek God's help to overcome fear, suspicion and inflexibility so your attitude will be one of openness, acceptance and trust. Are you worried that this attitude will be perceived as approval for other's sinful behavior? If so, you are still holding on to an attitude of fear, suspicion and inflexibility: why not trust God to move you? Then just watch and see how many new acquaintances come to know the same loving Savior you know. The result will be a change of attitude and lifestyle for those you meet.

Blessed are You, O God, King of the universe who brings the warmth of the sun every day and the refreshment of the rains. You bring forth food from the earth to nourish our bodies and you call us to serve you with the strength you give. To those who are sick, I ask for healing, and for all who are stricken by sin I ask for the healing power of your forgiveness. In the Name above all names, Jesus Christ. AMEN!

***

Day 86

Christ is the visible image of the invisible God. He existed before anything was created and is supreme over all creation, for through him God created everything in the heavenly realms and on earth. He made the things we can see and the things we can't see – such as thrones, kingdoms, rulers, and authorities in the unseen world. Everything was created through him and for him. Col. 1:15-16 (NLT)

"In this life there is no finished symphony. Because of that we will, on this side of eternity, always be lonely, restless, and incomplete." Fr. Ron Rolheiser

Today is a day full of opportunity! God is the God who offers opportunities for life, joy, peace and celebration. Did you see the word 'offers'? Yes, God offers us many things and it is up to us to decide whether we will accept or reject them. Jesus said; "Come to me, all of you who are weary and carry heavy burdens, and I will give you rest." (Matt 11:28 NLT) and with these words He offered us a great opportunity. The opportunity is to use the burdens we carry as the building blocks for our life. Consider every challenge a brick; a difficult daughter or son may be a brick as you build your life. A coworker that just won't give you a break, a car that repeatedly breaks down, or a deep financial pit you just can't seem to get out of; all can be bricks with which you build your life. But the bricks have to get to the foundation before they can be used for building. Jesus says, "Let me carry them for you!"

There was once a man named Kent who always considered it a privilege to live in God's world. He suffered from cerebral palsy from birth. Many people would tell the stories of how he was so determined as a child to go to the front of the church with his friends to sing a song that he would literally drag himself on the floor, using only his arms, and up into a chair so he could be with his friends. I have often imagined him as a real life Forrest Gump. When Kent grew a little older he was fitted with leg braces and he forced himself to walk, slowly but surely he accomplished his goal. But one thing Kent always carried with him was, what I believe, the most important tool in his quest to walk and function in life. The one thing that enabled everyone to know he was for real, and that was his smile as he would push the broken words out of his mouth; "Je-sus...lo-ves...m-e...a-nd...you too!"

Once Kent was very ill, He was in the hospital suffering with a bowel obstruction. His pain was unbearable but he still responded the same way as always when I walked into his hospital room. His face lit up and he smiled from ear to ear and said; "Je-sus...lo-ves...m-e...a-nd...you too!"

Very few can say they have carried a burden as heavy as Kent's burden. Very few people, me included, respond to the burdens in life the way Kent did. But everyone who is able to acknowledge faith in God as the mortar that hold the bricks of life in place will

163

eventually come to know life eternal and the place where the finished symphony is played for eternal life in joy, peace and celebration.

Holy Christ, lead me today in the path of your choosing. For my health I pray for strength and restoration, for my spirit I pray for blessing and guidance. Expand the boundaries of my life for you, and protect me from discouragement and evil attacks upon my desire to serve you faithfully. By you I am always made strong, through forgiveness of my sins and my desire to follow you. AMEN!

***

Day 87

For you are all children of God through faith in Christ Jesus. And all who have been united in Christ in baptism have put on Christ, like putting on new clothes. There is no longer Jew of Gentile, slave or free, male and female. For you are all one in Christ Jesus. Gal. 3:26-28 (NLT)

The new life of a Christian is a life lived for Christ, no longer for self-preservation and personal gain or success. There is a new center of life, when Christ enters our life. When Christ is present everything is filtered through God's will, not ours. But it is important not to set ourselves up for failure and fall into the trap of our human condition. You see, we often want change and we want it now! The reality in which we live is this, change that happens rapidly due to our personal will, is change that does not last. Only God can affect instant change, we must travel, or journey, into a changed life.

So putting on Christ must be a daily activity, one that fosters our regular process of change.

The regular process of change may be witnessed by those around us as they observe how different our behavior is after Christ comes into our life. People see that our smile is different than before. Strangers are greeted with a genuine smile of acceptance, not a smirk of suspicion. Our friends notice that we seem to welcome strangers into our circle of acquaintance rather than avoid them. This new behavior is a sure sign of putting on Christ, different from the rest of the world. With the smile comes a definite desire to reach out rather than to stay reserved and withdrawn. Reaching out is exactly what Christ has done for us and we reciprocate by reaching out to others, we become the helpers, no longer the helped.

Putting on Christ compels us to engage people and we find ourselves becoming more sensitive to their needs. We are more likely to lend a helping hand to the stranger leaving the grocery who cannot carry all her bags. Or, maybe we see a young parent struggling to open a door with a child in his arms, so we open the door for him. We engage people like never before, because Christ is in us, we have put on Christ. Engaging people require us to suspend judgment just as Christ did for us. That doesn't mean we approve, it means that for a time we see the need as greater than the person's behavior or place in society. Did not Christ do the same for all, when on the cross?

Putting on Christ each day allows us to behave different and there is a tremendous benefit to all this, we become more expressive, more generous, and more invitational. Think for a moment as you prepare to begin, or finish this day. Do not all of these attribute above clearly describe how Christ is dealing with you? Smiling, reaching out, engaging, suspending judgment, expressing concern and love, generosity, and inviting us to come closer, all describe the love of Jesus Christ coming to us. As Paul said; "You are all one in Christ Jesus."

Good and Gracious God; my heart is filled with appreciation and praise as a new day begins in Your Kingdom. As one who deserves not one of your blessings I am in awe that your love is so clear for me. I pray for your continued forgiveness and understanding, and I dedicate my life to you this day. All of this as I know my life is so much more fortunate with you, therefore I will serve you and I ask you to put me to the work of your calling today. In the Blessed name of Jesus I pray. AMEN!

***

Day 88

For you have been called to live in freedom, my brothers and sisters. But don't use your freedom to satisfy your sinful nature. Instead, use your freedom to serve one another in love. Gal 5:13 (NLT)

"Let it be your business to keep your mind in the presence of the Lord." Brother Lawrence

When the people called Israel set out to leave Egypt they were following God who represented freedom to them. Moses was the only one who knew the destination of their journey, the rest were followers who placed their trust in the stories of their elders and ultimately in Moses. But Moses, like the elders whose stories of Joseph and Jacob, practiced a very important spiritual habit which the people of Israel would take decades, some say centuries, to learn. They knew the presence of God, daily.

For the newly independent Israelites God provided clear signs of presence. The Bible tells us, in Exodus, that God went before them as a pillar of smoke in the day and a pillar of fire by night, two clearly visible signs of God's presence. Moses reminded the people every day of their journey that the Lord their God was leading them to a Promised Land, the land of their father Jacob. And so their journey continued, not without challenges and near disaster in which they nearly turned around. In fact, there was a time of such absolute disobedience that God destined them to wander long enough for an entire generation to pass away. But the signs of God's presence never left them. Smoke by day and fire by night, even Moses and his brother Aaron can be considered signs of God's presence, and the Commandments, the Ark of the Covenant, quail and manna, even the traveling Tabernacle which God commanded them to build were all signs of God's presence.

Today, four to six thousand years later we still have a tendency to miss seeing the signs of God's presence. What signs has faith in the One true God made evident in today's world? Where are the pillars of smoke and fire? The answer is all around us. Were it not for the Judeo-Christian faith churches, synagogues, hospitals and schools would not exist. Yes, through the Scriptural message all these things have come into being. So many concepts of relationships have all been God's idea, helping, supporting and nurturing one another in everyday life is also God's idea handed to us.

So today, no matter what life brings you, as you walk this journey of freedom, see the pillar of smoke and fire. Know the presence of God in your life; make it your business to keep the presence of God in your life. And tonight, when the sun goes down and darkness overtakes the day, remember the Light of Christ is within and around you everywhere.

God, I pray for a new sense of your presence today. Give me clear vision as my journey through this life continues and please remind me of my true destination, to dwell for all eternity in your home. For now, give me direction for ministry and service, show me the places and the people you call me to and give me the strength and health to properly serve you. Forgive my sin as I forgive others. In Jesus' blessed name I pray. AMEN!

***

Day 89

Therefore go and make disciples of all nations, baptizing them in the name of the Father and the Son and the Holy Spirit. Teach these new disciples to obey the commands I have given you. And be sure of this: I am with you always, even to the end of the age. Matt 28:19-20 (NLT)

Following the passion God places in each of us has always been a challenge. We are met with many reasons to ignore any inner desire toward outward expressions of our faith. We find ourselves sort of "singing in the shower" when it comes to our passions for ministry and service. Many pastors will tell of running away from their call to ministry year after year, until they finally surrender to the inner passion to preach. Tex Sample once said; "Holding back on a call to preach is like vomiting. You can hold it in for a while, but eventually it comes out uncontrollably!" Our God given passion for ministry is intended to come out, but the world is very good at discouraging and intimidating!

Peter Drucker once told a story about a forest full of animals. One day the supreme animal council was meeting to decide what they should do with their young. The mother bear suggested they start a school so they could collectively train their young for success in life. And, it would help their behavior as well. Everyone thought it was an excellent idea. So, they asked wise old Owl to be their superintendent, he accepted and wolf, bobcat and fox agreed to be the school board. Next, they needed funding to pay their teachers, so they got a government grant! They we all set and school opened right on schedule, September 1. They had running class, swimming class, flying class, and hunting class.

Near the end of the first semester, just before the Hibernation Break, the animal school board decided that they should evaluate all the students. One by one, the students were evaluated and one student in particular seemed to be getting a few bad grades, young rabbit. So the school board called young rabbit to the office to discuss his grades. "Rabbit," said Owl, "We have noticed you are doing an excellent job in running class, but you are failing in swimming, hunting, and flying." Everyone agreed that something had to be done, after all, their government grant was based on successful education and they simply could not have a failing student in their school. Owl continued; "So rabbit, what we are going to do is take you out of running class and double your time in flying class, we believe swimming and hunting will also be improved if you don't spend any time on running."

Well, rabbit responded as you or I would, he dropped out of the school! Here's the moral, it is not wise or productive to ask someone to do something for which they have no natural God given ability, it will accomplish only one thing, discouragement. That's why God puts passion within your heart for something. What is your passion, what do you really love to do? When the Holy Spirit is the guide our passions are used for the good of God's Kingdom, whatever the passion may be. Writing, singing, caring, helping, preaching, teaching, walking, running, swimming, flying (in planes) are all potential passions that may be used for the glory of God. And remember, owls are really not that smart, all they can do is ask one question: "WHO?"

Awaken me, O God, to the many needs of this world. Awaken my heart so I will know your love and know those who need love. Awaken my mind so I will gain understanding of Your Word and Your precepts. Awaken my feet so I will go where you send me and my hands so I will do what you call me to doing. In the Name of Christ my Lord, AMEN!

**

Day 90

God the Father knew you and chose you long ago, and his Spirit has made you holy. As a result, you have obeyed him and have been cleansed by the blood of Jesus Christ. May God give you more and more grace and peace. 1 Pt 1:2 (NLT)

"One does not become holy all at once." Brother Lawrence

In the book "Images of the Church in Mission" John Driver describes, what he calls, the churches role in the world as salt, light and the mountaintop city. Driver points out that all three metaphors are drawn from the Old Testament, interesting that most Christians today consider them New Testament as we associate them with Jesus' teaching. It is vital for us to remember that the Bible is one story of faith, not two, and that Jesus taught with the text we know today as the Old Testament, in His time, the Law and the Prophets with the Psalms etc.

"Salt of the Covenant" is referred to in Num. 18:19 (Driver, pg. 171) undoubtedly for its principles of preservation, as well as seasoning. Interesting though, salt also has corrosive effect if it is left to itself. One must wonder if that too is part of the metaphor for the actions of God's people. We can either use the gifts God has blessed us with and see the good result in the world, or ignore them and watch as the world crumbles in decay.

The servant of God is to be the light to the nations (Driver, pg.172) which is referenced, again in the Old Testament "I have given you as a covenant to the people, alight to the nations." (Is 42:6) The light the people will take notice of and also be drawn to, as in Is 60:19. Here again, the light has the potential for both positive and negative influence. The light, when used by the believer, can have the positive affect of attracting others to God almost as a moth is drawn to the light in the darkness because of the contrast. However, if the light is not used as a guiding beacon in process of a journey, like the moth those who are attracted will either be burned by the light, eaten by a predator of the night, or simply waste the potential of a lifetime.

The mountaintop city is also an Old Testament image; "The mountain of the Lord's house shall be established as the highest of the mountains...all nations [all peoples] shall stream to it" (Is 2:2-3, Micah 4:1-2, Zech. 8:20, 22.) (Driver, pg. 173) Again, the mountaintop city can have a positive and a negative effect. If the people of the city, God's people, are serving to help others gain entrance into the city then there is positive result. But, if the inhabitants of the city wall themselves off from the rest of the world, the people on the outside face hardship, struggle and eventual destruction. As with the previous two metaphors, the negative potential is always present and the deciding factor comes down to the people of God and how; salt, light and the mountaintop are used.

In Driver's book he draws this all together by writing about the use of the plural pronoun "you" in Matthew 5. In the Beatitudes, "Blessed are you..." is not referring to individuals, not to me specifically or you specifically but to the people of God. And when Jesus says; "You are the salt of the earth...You are the light of the world...let your good deeds shine for all to see..." (Matt 5:13, 14, 16) He is calling all believers to the positive impact of salt, light and visibility. So there we are, we have our road map, our GPS co-ordinance, and it's time to push the "go" button

Dear God, I begin this day looking for places to grow; in my intellect, in my heart and in my spirit, I desire growth. As Your Word sets the seed and the experiences of this day fertilize the ground, may Your Holy Spirit be the refreshing water and nourishment I require. As I grow in you I see my needs and my shortcomings so please forgive me and set me on the path of your choosing. In Christ I pray, AMEN!

***

Day 91

You love him even though you have never seen him. Though you do not see him now, you trust him; and you rejoice with a glorious, inexpressible joy. The reward for trusting him will be the salvation of your souls. 1 Pt 1:8-9 (NLT)

"We can't convince (much less convict) other people of their need to know God that is the work of the Holy Spirit." Richard Peace

Have you ever stopped to consider how many people have played a role in your coming to know the love of God? Yes we all know the role of the local church and committed pastors and teachers, that friend who invited you to come to a small group, or Bible study, or Sunday school class, all of these are indeed important in helping you find your way to God. But there are others whom we don't often credit. What about the people who prayed for you when you were just a newborn and hadn't the slightest idea they were doing so? Those people may have been your parents, grandparents, other extended family, neighbors and friends of your family, church members and pastors as well. John Wesley referred to these prayers as instruments of prevenient grace, surrounding you with the presence of God's Holy Spirit and protecting you.

And there are still others, like the people we read about in the Bible; Abraham, Moses, Ruth, David, Elijah, Simeon, Pricilla, Peter, James and Paul just to name a few. And what about Stephen, the first recorded martyr in the Bible. Stephen's death in Acts 7 served as the catalyst for what is often referred to as the "spontaneous expansion of the church." But Stephen's death had even greater impact than just scattering the Christians from Jerusalem to the rest of the world, Stephen's death left a mark on the mind and heart of the Apostle Paul. Paul, then called Saul, was involved in the condemnation of Stephen and as St. Augustine said; "The Church owes Paul to the prayer of Stephen."

When faced with death as the reward for his faith, Stephen was filled with the glory of the Holy Spirit and his prayer was one of thanksgiving, not one of fear and pleading. A young man named Saul witnessed that moment, and later when confronted with the Living Christ, Saul became Paul, God's apostle to the Gentiles, you and me! Once again, have you ever stopped to consider how many people have played a role in your coming to know the love of God?

Great and Almighty God, I thank you for the many ways you show yourself to me each day. I hear you in the songs of the birds, I feel you in the gentle breezes and the warmth of the sun. I know the firmness of your strength as my feet trod the soil of the earth and I know you are near as the challenges come into my life, and I lean of you. I give you praise and thanksgiving for all you have given me and continue to bring me. In Christ's Name I pray; AMEN!

***

Day 92

And remember that the heavenly Father to whom you pray has no favorites. He will judge or reward you according to what you do. So you must live in reverent fear of him during your time as "foreigners in the land." For you know that God paid a ransom to save you from the empty life you inherited from your ancestors. And the ransom he paid was not mere gold or silver. 1 Pt 1:17-18 (NLT)

What exactly does God expect of us? Peter's statement; "judge or reward..." carries all sorts of implications. Because of our English translations the word judge, when used in the scripture, is considered synonymous with condemnation. I don't believe that is correct because it distorts the entire image of God Christ gives us. I believe a better word would be "measure", God will measure and reward us according to what we do. If we do very little we should expect little, if we do a great deal we can expect a great reward, however, we should NEVER think our work in the Kingdom of God is based on rewards, our work is based soundly in gratitude for what God has done for us!

God has always had high expectation for His people. In the Old Testament when the Jewish people were taken from their homes into exile: once by the Assyrians and once by the Babylonians, then later as servants and teachers for the Romans, something very interesting began to happen. This phenomenon is referred to as the diaspora or dispersion of the Jewish people around the world. During this time we see the earliest missionary efforts begin to develop.

It was by the Jewish people's practice of their faith that many new converts to Judaism came to know God. Their worship was different from the people in the lands they found themselves in. The Jews proclaimed one true God and they stood on that foundation no matter what threats or temptations they faced. They proclaimed obedience to God's law as the one true path to spiritual salvation, rather than multiple paths toward eternal security. And thirdly; they shared their conviction that hope for humankind would only be found in faithful worship of one true God and absolute obedience to His law. Do you see a pattern here?

The result, the reward if you will, was that the Jewish faith grew in numbers at a greater rate than that of the birth rate. What does that tell us? Evangelism was alive and well and the mission of God's people then, as well as now, was and is to tell the nations of God's great mercies and grace and the reward is all God's. What do we get out of it? The knowledge that one day we will hear the words from God; "Well done, good and faithful servant..."

Lord God Almighty; on this Your Holy Day, may my life be filled with love, joy, peace and self-control as I walk this path for you. Today I pray for the strength and fortitude to carry on as I serve you and may my actions and thoughts multiply your desires. God, I ask for your forgiveness of my sins, sins of thought or deed, and I pray for the forgiveness of all your children today. In Christ's Name; AMEN!

***

Day 93

And you are living stones that God is building into his spiritual temple. What's more, you are his holy priests. Through the mediation of Jesus Christ, you offer spiritual sacrifices that please God. As the Scriptures say, "I am placing a cornerstone in Jerusalem, chosen for great honor, and anyone who trusts him will never be disgraced." 1 Pt 2:5-6 (NLT)

"The greatest form of praise is the sound of consecrated feet seeking out the lost and helpless." Rev. Dr. Billy Graham

Very often when we think of the image of living stones we focus on an inanimate object coming to life. But that is not God's message to us in this metaphor; God's message has to do with the process of bringing us from death to life. In the Old Testament the Hebrew word *oikos* is found, it means family or race, so we would say the human *oikos* was created by God. [In the English language we have many words with one use, in the Hebrew there are many uses for one word] This *oikos* was created as an individual that soon felt the need for community so as God created the first, God created the second from the first and set into motion the multiplying process we call procreation, the process of bringing life into the world.

In the New Testament the same word, *oikos*, is used for house and household, stay with me now, so we see God's intention that the existence of humanity is to be life in community. In a sense we do not exist to be alone, we exist for the purpose of being in a family, with others. Very few people can thrive alone, there are always other people who play a role in the process, and we call this edification. And, wouldn't you know it, the word used in the New Testament for edification is, wait for it; *oikodomeo*. The created is created to be part of a family; the family is created to be part of the wider community which is the Church for Christians.

The Church is nothing more than a continuation of the concept of the People of God we read of in the Old Testament. In Jeremiah we read; "I will set my eyes upon them (*oikos*) for good and I will bring them back to this land." (Jer. 24:5) Notice it says "them" not him or her, demonstrating that God works with the community, the Church. Another example is, "I will manifest my holiness among you (*oikos*) in the sight of the nations…" (Ezek 20:44) Again, the word for "you" is not singular but plural. Jesus uses the same word in the Sermon on the Mount when he speaks the Beatitudes; "Blessed are you…" speaking to all God's people not an individual. So, when we speak of ourselves as the hands and feet of God we speak of the many, not just our own, and we acknowledge our need for the Church, the Body of Christ, of which we are a part of the whole.

Lord Almighty, Maker of heaven and earth, today I stand ready for your call, assign me to your work and use me as you will. O God, I pray for all your servants, shield and protect them as they go into places and situations that threaten their lives as well as their faith. I ask you; give to every one of them the strength and fortitude of worthy soldiers in Your Army of Grace and may your will be done in every way. Provide, also, the health and peace required for stamina in your service so that all who are yet to believe will see you in each life. In the name of the One Christ I pray this, AMEN!

***

Day 94

For God called you to do good, even if it means suffering, just as Christ suffered for you. He is your example, and you must follow his steps. He never sinned, nor even deceived anyone. He did not retaliate when he was insulted, nor threaten revenge when he suffered. He left his case in the hands of God, who always judges fairly. 1 Pt 2:21-23 (NLT)

The meaning of praise is always relative. I remember seeing a sign on the wall of a mess hall at a church camp reading; "Complaints are to the Devil what praise is to God!" I guess the emphasis is on affirmation here. Praise is affirmation, it is a sign of thanks, it is a sign of appreciation and it is a sign of acceptance. Who doesn't want to be praised? Well, I can tell you, God wants to hear our praise in any form we wish to offer.

Praise comes in form of prayer, such as prayers of thanks giving. Praise comes in form of action, such as responding to God's call to mission or ministry. Praise come in form of singing, as we sing songs and hymns about God, and in more contemporary settings, we sing

179

songs to God. In the early years of the development of the United States, the churches and the many Christian movements and associations were pivotal to establishing the character of a new nation. One old camp meeting song, in an 1807 song book went like this; "The Methodists were preaching like thunder all about. At length I went amongst them, to hear them groan and shout. I thought they were distracted, such fools I'd never seen. They'd stamp and cramp and tremble, and wail and cry and scream!"

Some would think this little song described craziness, but others would say it describes a group of people so full of praise it could not be contained. I think we should always, as Peter wrote; leave the "case in the hands of God, who always judges fairly." After all, the praise is given to God; why not let God decide if it is good or bad?

Precious Lord, I ask you to set my feet upon the path of your choosing, today. May my decisions be clearly set in your will, and may my desire be yours. I ask you to heal all who are sick or injured today, comfort those who grieve and continue to love the unlovable. And God; I ask you to make my life as yours, so I will also love where no one loves. In Jesus' name I pray, AMEN!

***

Day 95

Finally, all of you should be of one mind. Sympathize with each other. Love each other as brothers and sisters. Be tenderhearted, and keep a humble attitude. Don't repay evil for evil. Don't retaliate with insults when people insult you. Instead, pay them back with a blessing. That is what God has called you to do, and will bless you for it. 1 Pt 3:8-9 (NLT)

"Continue, then, always with God; it is the only support and comfort for your affliction." Brother Lawrence

There is an episode in Mash, the "70's" television series about the Korean war, where Hawkeye, the central character in the series, is traveling by himself on his way to a few days of R&R in Seoul. Along the road he encounters a Chinese soldier who appears to take him prisoner, so at gunpoint his captor takes him to a young Chinese boy who has been shot. At first glance the boy looks very young and the impression is that he may even be the son of the other soldier. The language barrier is overcome by inferences and Hawkeye begins to care for the wounds the young boy has, all the while talking in English as the soldier barks orders in Chinese. Hawkeye knows his life depends on saving the life of the critically wounded boy.

Then something profound happens, Hawkeye's instincts begin to overwhelm his immediate sense of danger and he begins to bark orders to the soldier. As the young boy slips closer and closer to death, Hawkeye demands action from his captor as he works faster and faster with one thing in mind; save a life that is slipping away. And then suddenly, the boy stops breathing.

Hawkeye begins feverishly trying to revive him; respirations through the trachea tube and violently pumping his chest. But the life of the young Chinese boy, once a soldier, slips away into eternity. Now returns the fear Hawkeye initially felt, surely he would be the next to die because he failed.

But the soldier who had taken him by gunpoint, and had threatened him with death if he did not help the boy apparently sensed that Hawkeye was genuinely concerned with saving the boy's life, not his own. The soldier picked up his rifle, Hawkeye cringed, and then the soldier took his bayonet off the rifle and began digging a grave for his son. Hawkeye picked up his knapsack and started to walk away. He stopped, turned and began digging the grave with his captor, both realizing their common bond the horrors of war had brought. They were of one mind!

We share a war, in this world. It is a war, as Paul writes, "not with governments and armies, but with sin," (Rom 7:23.) We share this common enemy with all of God's people so: why not begin to fight this common enemy together?

God of the Universe; today I pray to you for comfort and strength to persevere, amidst every challenge in this life, you sustain and send forth an army of servants, serving you by serving others. Cleanse my thoughts toward all people today and make my spirit right as I journey through this life. And, I ask for opportunities to forgive as you have forgiven me. In the glorious and gentle name of Christ I pray, AMEN!

***

Day 96

Therefore, humble yourselves under God's power so that he may raise you up in the last day. Throw all your anxiety onto him, because he cares about you. 1 Pt 5:6-7 (CEB)

There is one, and only one, pivotal moment in every believer's spiritual life and that is the moment they are convinced of their sin. Nothing else matters, there is no other moment greater, there is absolutely nothing more important in our eternal nature than the very moment we arc able to say to God; "Be merciful to me, a sinner!" (Lk 18:13)This is why many Christians experience much frustration in witnessing to their family and friends. Those who have not come to acceptance of their sin have no basis on which to receive Christ as their Savior. Yes, they (we) are always willing to unload our burdens, even if on God for the moment, but we are reluctant to release them completely. The string that keeps us tied to our burdens is our inability to admit our sinfulness. The old; "I'm OK, you're OK" syndrome has become our "SIN-drome"!

When you became free, and filled with the love of Christ you admitted your sinfulness. You were, as John Wesley put it, justified by your faith, and at that moment sanctification began. Sanctification is the process of becoming what God intends us to become, a fruit bearing disciple. Think of it as a cleansing process, a washing of our souls, so to speak. But, without acknowledgement of sin sanctification is an empty bucket of cycles from sin to forgiveness and back again. As the Bible says, "You are saved by God's grace because of your faith." (Eph. 2:8)So the first step is faith, not repentance, repentance comes after faith and then faith leads to justification and sanctification, but without faith there is no true repentance. So, we're not 'saved' we are 'justified' before God when we repent. Clear as mud?

Now, imagine this, if we get confused about the correlation between; faith, justification and sanctification, how much more do our pre-Christian friends? Maybe this is why our witnessing is so difficult, we have been asking them to have faith without knowing what sin is. And we know if we go about telling everyone they are sinners we will soon be without an audience. Let's start here; live a life so full of goodness and mercy that others will look at us and think; "I want a life like that!" Live a life full of forgiveness, a life of absolute integrity so we can demonstrate the fact that we are different a contrast if you will. Then, I believe we will be able to respond to those we hope to bring to Christ, when their burden becomes unbearable we will be there to help free them, their sin will be visible to them and we can show them Christ who will take the burden away! So, don't worry about defining sin for others, simply live the life that exposes sin, and conquer it!

O God, who knows my needs and opens forth your hand to provide, guide me in your Way today so that my faith will grow and my spirit will be strong. Remind me, again, of your wonderful works and the many times you have reached into my life and delivered me. And God, please continue to forgive me, in my many mistakes and sins, and send me to situations which require me to forgive so I will know the value and power of your true forgiveness. I ask you for health, wholeness and happiness in Jesus' name, AMEN!

***

Day 97

The more you grow like this, the more productive and useful you will be in your knowledge of our Lord Jesus Christ. But those who fail to develop in this way are shortsighted or blind, forgetting that they have been cleansed from their old sins. 2 Pt 1:8-9 (NLT)

"The ultimate reality which is the object of all our search for truth has been made present in history in the person and work of Jesus Christ." Lesslie Newbigin

Our relationship with God is based on a solid, and true commitment called a covenant. A covenant is not a contract, as it has sometimes been explained. A covenant is a mutual commitment, a statement of intention, an absolute agreement grounded in spirit not practice. In other words, the party making the initial covenant does not depend on the second party to deliver, a covenant is solid. Covenant is also grounded in relationship, not performance, so our covenant relationship with God is firmly planted in God's Holy Spirit.

Our covenant relationship with God clearly communicates that the business of the Church, our business, is too important to leave to chance. There is no 'auto pilot' for the Church; we must be actively engaged in carrying on the mission of making disciples of Jesus

Christ. Our covenant relationship with God communicates our desire to care for one another. We all need support and we are all sharing this life in Christ, therefore we are the logical means of support for one another. And because of the covenant relationship we are all accountable to one another, setting examples for all who see what we do, and in turn we then are privileged to share our covenant relationship with all people.

Living in covenant relationship is a process. This is how we remain in Christ, as God nurtures our lives, forgives our sin, and resets our spirit. Through Christ we are given a second chance, and as many chances as is necessary to build our spiritual life to the point of strength that then becomes our way of life. Walking with the Spirit becomes walking in the Spirit and we then will the things God wills! Go ahead, get out there today and give it a "GROW", see how God will bless you beyond all expectations.

Lord God Almighty, thank you for being everything I need when I am in need. When I need strength, you are strong. When I am confused and need direction, you are sure. When I need forgiveness, you are compassionate. And when I need healing, you are the Great Physician who makes me whole. AMEN!

***

Day 98

But you must not forget this one thing, dear friends: A day is like a thousand years to the Lord, and a thousand years is like a day. The Lord isn't really being slow about his promise, as some people think. No, he is being patient for your sake. He does not want anyone to be destroyed, but wants everyone to repent. 2 Pt 3:8-9 (NLT)

"I beseech you; comfort yourself with him, who is the only physician of all our maladies. He is the Father of the afflicted, always ready to help us." Brother Lawrence

Clear sight is always best; obstacles, turns and curves in the road, walking up or down steps, and even in making decisions about the future all require clear vision in order to be safe and successful. Clear vision also helps us in everyday life by allowing our purpose to be fulfilled, in other words; knowing where I'm going is going to make every step productive because my purpose is not blurred by any spiritual astigmatism. Jesus said; "The lamp of the body is the eye. If therefore your eye is good, your whole body will be full of light." (Matt 6:22) Clearly focused attention on Christ provides for a smooth journey through life, regardless how many problems or setbacks we may encounter.

But when we lose focus on Christ and begin giving our attention to other things like; money, success, and self, we will begin experiencing a loss of faith. Jesus went on to say, in Matthew 6, the Sermon on the Mount, that when we give attention to anything but God we will effectively be serving that as our master. He was referring to money when he said; "You cannot serve God and mammon. Mammon was a reference to the Greek god of money. Does this mean God does not want you to have money? Absolutely not, it means God wants all of us to be good stewards of His money He has placed in our care. Money is a tool for the ministry and mission of God therefore, when I am blessed with money it is for the purpose of serving God. Money in the hands of a Christian is an opportunity to serve, so ask today: "What does the Master want me to do with this money opportunity today?"

O God, from whom all things come, I pray you will reach into the lives of all who struggle today and lift their spirits beyond their suffering. For those who are sick, please heal them, for those who grieve, please comfort them, and for all who sin, please forgive us. By your majesty and power you require my praise and I love you in all you do. In the name of the Holy One from Nazareth, Jesus Christ, AMEN!

***

Day 99

I will sacrifice a voluntary offering to you; I will praise your name, O Lord, for it is good. For you have rescued me from my troubles and helped me to triumph over my enemies. Ps. 54:6-7 (NLT)

Exactly what is a voluntary offering today? We don't sacrifice animals so would we burn a pile of money, or a car, or our new clothes? Probably not, but in our Christian culture we have come to associate time as perhaps our most valuable possession. Cat Stevens sang; "If I could take time in a bottle, the first thing I'd like to do..." making the point of how valuable time is and yet how it is not ours! Maybe time is a good sacrifice, a good voluntary offering to God in the twenty first century after all.

I believe this is why Jesus often spoke of what needs to be done in the world; Christ knew time was our greatest asset. He could have easily waved his hand and taken care of every need in the world, but he did not. Why would the King of the universe simply point out the problems and then leave? The answer is this, God's will is for us to be the ones who do the good works so He gave us time, Jesus was merely issuing the "work order" so to speak. In Matthew 25, beginning with the 31st verse, Jesus gives what is commonly referred to as The Great Compassion. He puts himself in the shoes of the hungry, the sick, the poor and naked, and the prisoner and says "You ministered to me." But the answer came, "When did we minister to you?" His reply, "That which you did for the least of these, you did for me." (Matt 25:40) The apostle James also made this point for Jesus, after his ascension back to heaven, he wrote; "faith without deeds is dead." (Jas 2:26)

These are attention grabbing statements so what can we, 21st century Christians, do about this apparent assignment? Well, Ron Sider wrote a book called "Rich Christians in an Age of Hunger" and in the book he included what he called a Generous Christian Pledge. The pledge starts with this opening statement; "I pledge to open my heart to God's call to care as much about the poor as the Bible does." And within the remaining pledge there is a one sentence prayer; "Lord Jesus teach my heart to care about the poor." I think this pledge is a good starting point for us all.

Holy God, you have created the mountains, and the valleys; the rivers and the seas; the earth and the heavens. I praise Your Holy name. I give thanks for all you do for me and I ask you to walk with me along this journey, give me confidence and safe keeping as I go to the places you send me. Bless all who worship you this day and may Your Holy Will be done here and everywhere. AMEN!

***

Day 100

If you love me, obey my commandments. And I will ask the Father, and he will give you another Advocate, who will never leave you. He is the Holy Spirit, who leads into all truth. The world cannot receive him, because it isn't looking for him and doesn't recognize him. But you know him, because he lives in you now and later will be in you. Jn 14:15-17 (NLT)

"It is the Holy Spirit who opens our eyes to the liberating grace of God." H. Eddie Fox

Obeying God's commands is the one sign of complete faith, without faith God's commands are mere words. But some may say there are too many commands and it is impossible to keep them all. Well, "the place to start is where you are", as Yogi Berra would say. Every Christian is acquainted with, and many pre-Christians are also familiar with these words; "For God so loved the world, he gave is only Son, that whoever believes in him should not perish but have eternal life." (John 3:16) Let's unpack those words so we can obey God's commands through our understanding this very basic instruction.

FOR GOD: God has initiated all mission in this world. From the very moment of humanities fall from grace in the garden God has been coming after us. Remember how God, when walking through the garden after Adam and Eve had eaten from the Tree of Knowledge, said; "Adam, where are you?" (Gen 3:9) God has been a pursuing God ever since, wanting to find us, even when we are hiding.

SO LOVED: Most deities in world history have been vindictive and condemning, in response to disobedience. When the ancient Greeks spoke of people being unfaithful to their gods they described major destruction. Even the Bible story of Sodom and Gomorrah is believed to be a mixture of Hebrew and Egyptian conjecture. Why? Because the nature of God is love, not condemnation, in fact Jesus, Paul and Peter all described the only condemnation humanity faces is at our own hands when we choose not to believe.

THE WORLD: In God's eyes there are no boundaries, no borders between nations, no differences between ethnicities either. When Jesus spoke the words of John 3:16 he was speaking to Nicodemus, this must have rocked his Jewish centered life. God loves the world, as the song "Jesus Loves the Little Children" goes, "Red and yellow, black and white, all are precious in His sight!"

THAT HE GAVE: The foundation of the Judeo/Christian faith is sacrifice, from the beginning of our theological formation the issue of sacrifice, a response to God, has always been in the forefront. Because of this God had to make the final sacrifice, the life of Jesus Christ, the perfect sacrifice for all human sin, past, present and future. Now, it is our turn, our response to God for forgiving our sins is to give to the world, the nations, all people, just as God has given to us.

HIS ONE AND ONLY SON: Salvation is found nowhere else than in Christ. We may be very good at rationalizing our way toward other means of salvation, but we fail. If we are to accept the blessings of salvation as the Bible tells us, we must accept them through Christ.

THAT WHOEVER BELIEVES SHOULD NOT PERISH BUT HAVE ETERNAL LIFE: God's mission calls for a response: What will we do? God's mission is a warning to those who refuse to believe: Will we believe? God's mission is eternally significant for every person on the face of the earth: Will our relationship with Him produce a relationship with the rest of creation, red and yellow, black and white?

Come Holy Spirit come, come with the rush of the wind and the heat of the fire and burn within my heart a new desire; a desire to love you, to serve you, and to follow you. Come Holy Spirit come. Today I seek your direction, as well as, companionship. I seek comfort, as well as healing and wholeness. And I seek forgiveness for without it I am nothing. In Christ's loving name I pray. AMEN!

***

Post-Script

It is my prayer that God has used this last 100 days to grow His Spirit within your heart. Perhaps my sharing these few stories and anecdotes with you has served to germinate some seeds of the Spirit within. And I do hope and pray you have continued to develop your habit of spending time with God every day. If you would like to continue this discipline I would be honored, and blessed if you continue in the Rivers of Eden Series with Volume II. May God continue to richly bless your spiritual journey!

In Christ,

James Craig Noggle

77,99/25
69/26:39,42
54,60,89/28:
19-20
19/28:20

MARK
51/2:17
36/12:29-31
6/14:36
58/15:33-
35,37
50/16:15-16

LUKE
56/4:4,8,30
27/4:5-8
37/5:10
60/10:21
38/10:25-37
8/12:22-24
83/13:10-14
83/13:21
40/14:28
1/16:1
96/18:13
75/23:34

JOHN
29/3:6-8
63,100/3:16
JOHN
11/4:36
71/11:4,6-7
10/12:23-25
48/13:15-17

100/14:15-
17
1/16:1
14,81/16:33
76/17:18-20
40/21:15

ACTS
77/2:38
91/7
48/8:32-33
18/11:23
57/28:27

ROMANS
63/3:23
4/5:17,21
95/7:23
79/10:9
63/10:13
9,82/12:1-2

1
Corinthians
46/13:4-7
66/13:12-13

2
Corinthians
45/2:15-16

GALATIAN
S
87/3:26-28
88/5:13
38/5:14-16
55/6:15b

Ephesians
22/1:3-4
49/1:17-19
96/2:8
61/6:5-6

Philippians
12/2:3-5
81/2:16

Colossians
79/1:6
86/1:15-16
37/3:12-14

1 Thess.
64/3:9-12
41/5:14-18

1 Timothy
28,74/1:12-
14

HEBREWS
78/12:1

JAMES
63,81/1:2-4
99/2:26
53/3:13

1 PETER
90/1:2
19/1:6-7
91/1:8-9
92/1:17-18

196

93/2:5-6
57/2:15-17
94/2:21-23
95/3:8-9
96/5:6-7

2 PETER
30/1:3-4
59/1:3-4
97/1:8-9
98/3:8-9
54/3:14

1 JOHN
73/2:7-8
JUDE
33/1:24-25

Revelation
50/3:20
47/22:16-17

20156901R00114

Made in the USA
Middletown, DE
17 May 2015